MW00976951

.

A LETTER TO
THE BODY OF CHRIST
WHO WE ARE AND WHAT WE ARE ABOUT

TO ALL MY FELLOW MEMBERS
OF THE BODY OF CHRIST

JAMES KIM

A Letter to the Body of Christ:
Who We Are and What We Are About

Copyright © 2019 James Kim

Scripture taken from the NEW AMERICAN
STANDARD BIBLE®, Copyright © 1960,
1962, 1963, 1968, 1971, 1972, 1973, 1975, 1977,
1995 by The Lockman Foundation. Used by
permission. Italics in Scripture are added by the
author for emphasis.

ISBN13: 978-1-7084856-0-3
Printed in the United States of America

This book is to all my fellow members
of the body of Christ

So we, who are many, are one body in Christ,
and individually members one of another.
Romans 12:5

May we all be filled with the Holy Spirit, led by the Spirit,
and do all things by the Spirit who strengthens us.

When we rely on the Spirit of God in us to live through
us, He will surely lead us to live a life in Christ.

Contents

As I Write This Book

This book is written as a letter to everyone who is in the body of Christ. In this book, I would like to talk about who we are as believers in Christ and what we are to be about. The expression I use frequently in this book is "we." As you read this book, may the Holy Spirit show you all who belong in that expression "we."

May God use this book to show you the reason we were born into this world and the reason we live. May it direct our hearts to the Lord of all things in the heavens and the earth, the true son of God, our Savior Jesus Christ.

I pray that God would use this book from the first page to the last for our Lord Jesus Christ to be glorified with all glory in the heavens and the earth.

Let's remember that God, who created all things, lives and reigns today, and is working everywhere even in this very hour.

As our Lord Jesus Christ said many times, He is coming back soon. So I am writing this book with a heart like John's to "make ready the way of the Lord, make His paths straight!" In these last days, we ought to prepare ourselves, to be ready, and to be a voice of help and encouragement to prepare other members of the body of Christ as the Lord leads and directs our steps.

A voice is calling,
"Clear the way for the Lord in the wilderness;
Make smooth in the desert a highway for our God.
"Let every valley be lifted up,
And every mountain and hill be made low;
And let the rough ground become a plain,
And the rugged terrain a broad valley;
Then the glory of the Lord will be revealed,
And all flesh will see it together;
For the mouth of the Lord has spoken."
Isaiah 40:3-5

I pray the Lord would use this book as part of His wake-up call to His church. As I read and considered the Scriptures about the times we live in, they spoke to my heart and the Spirit confirmed that it is not time to fear and hide; but rather to rally His church, which is the body of Christ, to prepare ourselves as a bride who is making herself ready for her bridegroom to return soon. This is my heart in writing this book. We need to know who we are and what we are about.

There is much the Spirit is speaking to us in these last days. May the Lord bless you and speak to you whoever and wherever you are.

May our Savior, Jesus Christ, the KING OF KINGS and LORD OF LORDS, be glorified among us, through us, in us, and with us forever and ever. Amen.

Your brother and fellow member of the body of Christ,

James Kim
Memphis, Tennessee, U.S.A.

Preface

Please read the book of Genesis. From the creation, there are many mysteries we cannot fathom through modern science. God created everything by the Word. When God said, "Let there be light," there was light. When the Lord God formed man out of the dust of the ground and breathed the breath of life into him, man became a living being.

God created all things in the heavens and on the earth

because of His great will. He had His own purposes even before the creation. One of His purposes is for you and me as individual believers. His other purpose is for the corporate body of Christ, which is the church, and includes all those individual believers. In this book, I would like to share about the corporate body of Christ, which is the church, and what God purposed through that church. As we begin, let's look at these verses from the epistle to the Ephesians.

He made known to us the mystery of His will, according to His kind intention which He purposed in Him with a view to an administration suitable to the fullness of the times, that is, the summing up of all things in Christ, things in the heavens and things on the earth.

Ephesians 1:9-10

Some time ago, after I became a Christian and was born again, I believed that the most important event in my life was accepting Jesus Christ as my Savior. I still believe that is absolutely true. Around that same time I also thought that the will of God was to bring more people into His kingdom so that His Son Jesus Christ would receive all the glory with the Father, and that in doing so He would enlarge His kingdom by adding more citizens, more adopted sons with whom to enjoy His kingdom. While all of this is true, the Lord has been showing me that there is more. He has a bigger purpose for the corporate body of Christ, which includes all of us individual believers. This was to me a most remarkable revelation as I sought the Lord regarding who we are and what we are about. Truly, being saved by the grace of God is the greatest gift anyone of us can have in our lifetime here on earth. Having more people saved into God's kingdom through the blood of His Son Jesus Christ is surely a glorious redemption we all need to rejoice about, praise the Lord! But salvation by itself does not sum up all things in Christ. While Christ can be the Savior for mankind, and everyone who believes will enter into God's kingdom through Him, individual salvation does not itself sum up all things in Christ. What then are we to be about?

What is the purpose of our life together as the church?

Chapter 1
Ekklēsia, The Church

People often use the word "church" as they point to buildings with crosses or signs with names describing various affiliations or denominations. "Church" has come to mean a place of worship or a place where Christians gather. The word "church" has come to represent a physical building. This is very regrettable because it is far from the original meaning of the word "church." When you read the word "church" in this book, please do not think of it as a building or place. Please read with an open heart.

If we think of church as a building or place, we cannot escape the religious way of thinking that says we must be in one of those buildings or places to meet and worship God. For clarity, I will frequently add a Greek word, ekklēsia, when I use the word "church" to help us remember to consider its original and true meaning. "Ekklēsia" is the New Testament Greek word translated as "church" in English.

I desperately pray that the Holy Spirit would speak to all of us and show us the real meaning of "church" (ekklēsia) when our Lord Jesus and His apostles used that word during the first century. And I pray God's purpose would be accomplished through the church (ekklēsia) as He intended.

First of all, let's look at how our Lord Jesus used the word when He said "My church" in the Gospel of Matthew.

I also say to you that you are Peter, and upon this rock I will build My church; and the gates of Hades will not overpower it.
Matthew 16:18

Here is the first mention of the word "ekklēsia" in the Bible. Ekklēsia is a compound word from the preposition "ek" (meaning of, from, out of) and the verb "kaleo" (meaning to call). It literally means "called out ones" or "called ones." It is also understood as a gathering or an assembly of citizens or of the Israelites and contains the idea of a mass of people. So the word "ekklēsia" means people who were called out, assembled, or gathered as His people. It does not mean a building or place. This common misconception is why you may have felt very spiritual while in a building or place called a church but less spiritual or not spiritual at all as you got away from that building or place. Have you ever felt that your spirituality was determined by whether you showed up at those buildings or places called churches on Sunday but then you didn't feel too concerned with spirituality the rest of the week? Have you ever felt that you did the right thing by showing up and attending what we call a "church worship service," but walked away empty and dry spiritually? It is all because we think that the church is a building or place rather than realizing that we, the believers, are the church.

When our Lord Jesus said, "I will build My church." (Matt 16:18), He did not mean any building or religious place. He meant His people who are called, assembled, or gathered as the body of Christ, which is the church. After our Lord Jesus first spoke the word "church (ekklēsia)," this word appears more than one hundred times in the New Testament (exactly 112 times in the New American Standard Bible, which I use). Most of the time it is used simply to refer to the people, but there are a few passages that actually explain what the ekklēsia is. Let's look at a few of those Scriptures.

He is also head of the body, the church; and He is the beginning, the firstborn from the dead, so that He Himself will come to have first place in everything.
Colossians 1:18

Now I rejoice in my sufferings for your sake, and in my flesh I do my share on behalf of His body, which is the church, in filling up what is lacking in Christ's afflictions.
Colossians 1:24

In these verses, the body of Christ is called the church. It is not just saying the body is *like* the church; rather, that the body of Christ *is* the church. It is not saying that a part of the body is the church, or a part of the church is the body, but that the body and the church are completely one and equal and express the same thing. The Bible consistently refers to the body of Christ as the church. Let's look at some other verses that explain and describe the church (ekklēsia).

And He put all things in subjection under His feet, and gave Him as head over all things to the church, which is His body, the fullness of Him who fills all in all.
    Ephesians 1:22-23

For no one ever hated his own flesh, but nourishes and cherishes it, just as Christ also does the church, because we are members of His body.
    Ephesians 5:29-30

    In Colossians, Paul said that the body of Christ is the Church, but here he says it the opposite way. The church (ekklēsia) is the body of Christ. In other words, the church is Christ's body and Christ is the head of the church. His body is said to be the fullness of Him who fills all in all. Paul says that Christ's nurturing and protecting the church is the same as nurturing and protecting His own body. Thus, the body of Christ is the church and the church is the body of Christ. Let us always keep this in mind.

    There is also a verse in First Timothy that describes what the church is.

But in case I am delayed, I write so that you will know how one ought to conduct himself in the household of God, which is the church of the living God, the pillar and support of the truth.

1 Timothy 3:15

But Christ was faithful as a Son over His house—whose house we are, if we hold fast our confidence and the boast of our hope firm until the end.

Hebrews 3:6

Paul explains that the church is the household of God, the pillar and support of the truth. Here the word translated "household" is the Greek word "oikos," which in other parts of the New Testament is translated "family," "dwelling place," and even "descendants."

Do you remember how much work and wealth were put into building the Old Testament house of God, also known as the temple? How much effort and devotion were expended, even though it was impossible to fully achieve that with human hands. Building a house where God can dwell with men in eternity could not be realized. Therefore, our Lord Jesus Christ came to build that house where God would dwell, a house in God's own image, a place where God's desire to live with men could be fulfilled. And Christ Himself, His body, became the house where God will dwell with His people forever.

Jesus answered them, "Destroy this temple, and in three days I will raise it up." The Jews then said, "It took forty-six years to build this temple, and will You raise it up in three days?" But He was speaking of the temple of His body. So when He was raised from the dead, His disciples remembered that He said this; and they believed the Scripture and the word which Jesus had spoken.

John 2:19

The temple here speaks of Jesus Christ's body. And we who believe in Him are also born again into His body so that God can even dwell in believers' bodies as His temple.

Do you not know that you are a temple of God and that the Spirit of God dwells in you? If any man destroys the temple of God, God will destroy him, for the temple of God is holy, and that is what you are.

1 Corinthians 3:16-17

Or do you not know that your body is a temple of the Holy Spirit who is in you, whom you have from God, and that you are not your own? For you have been bought with a price: therefore glorify God in your body.

1 Corinthians 6:19-20

As you can see, the body of Christ which is the church is also the house of God, the dwelling place of God, and the family and descendants of God, which means His people. You must be born again into the body of Christ and possess within you His spiritual life to become a house of God, a dwelling place of God, God's family and descendants, and God's people.

He called the body of Christ as the church (ekklēsia), and the people of that body are the people of God who are God's house, God's family and descendants. Throughout all of this, God has established His sovereign will to call the born-again believers as His eternal dwelling place and as His own family and descendants to fulfill and accomplish what He had planned before creation. Praise the Lord who created all things as He intended and purposed!

Chapter 2
How the Body Can be the Church (Ekklēsia)

How can we truly be the church (ekklēsia), the body of Christ? That secret is revealed in 1 Corinthians 15.

But now Christ has been raised from the dead, the first fruits of those who are asleep. For since by a man came death, by a man also came the resurrection of the dead. For as in Adam all die, so also in Christ all will be made alive.
  1 Corinthians 15:20-22

So also is the resurrection of the dead. It is sown a perishable body, it is raised an imperishable body; it is sown in dishonor, it is raised in glory; it is sown in weakness, it is raised in power; it is sown a natural body, it is raised a spiritual body. If there is a natural body, there is also a spiritual body. So also it is written, "The first man, Adam, became a living soul." The last Adam became a life-giving spirit.
1 Corinthians 15:42-45

Anyone who believes the Bible and our Lord Jesus will know these verses speak of the risen Christ. We ought also to remind ourselves that, through the death and resurrection of our Lord Jesus Christ, His believers obtain new life in Him. In other words, we must be born again in Christ to be part of His body, to have new life. It is our Savior, Jesus Christ, who gives life to and gathers His believers into the church, the body of Christ.

For by one Spirit we were all baptized into one body, whether Jews or Greeks, whether slaves or free, and we were all made to drink of one Spirit.
1 Corinthians 12:13

It is definitely not attending a "church service" or

"Christian gatherings" in and of itself that makes you a part of the body of Christ. It clearly says that by one Spirit, we were all baptized into one body and were all made to drink of one Spirit.

But the one who joins himself to the Lord is one spirit with Him.
1 Corinthians 6:17

As it is written in First Corinthians, when each believer joins himself to the Lord, we are one spirit with the Lord and become a member of the body of Christ, which is the church.

So going to "church services" or Christian gatherings does not by itself mean we belong to the people there. Each of us has to be born again into the body of Christ by having faith in the death and resurrection of our Lord Jesus, and only through our faith in Him can we belong to the spiritual body of Christ that is the church.

This is why the building or place where we gather is not the church, rather all who believe are the church and members of Christ's spiritual body. Whenever and wherever we as believers are gathered, we would be called the church.

Let us look at some Scriptures where assemblies of believers are spoken as the church (ekklēsia) or churches.

So the church throughout all Judea and Galilee and Samaria enjoyed peace, being built up; and going on in the fear of the Lord and in the comfort of the Holy Spirit, it continued to increase.
Acts 9:31

I was still unknown by sight to the churches of Judea which were in Christ;
Galatians 1:22

Greet Prisca and Aquila, my fellow workers in Christ Jesus, who for my life risked their own necks, to whom not only do I give thanks, but also all the churches of the Gentiles; also greet the church that is in their house. Greet Epaenetus, my beloved, who is the first convert to Christ from Asia.
Romans 16:3-5

The churches of Asia greet you. Aquila and Prisca greet you heartily in the Lord, with the church that is in their house.
1 Corinthians 16:19

Now, brethren, we wish to make known to you the grace of God which has been given in the churches of Macedonia,
2 Corinthians 8:1

Greet the brethren who are in Laodicea and also Nympha and the church that is in her house.
Colossians 4:15

And to Apphia our sister, and to Archippus our fellow soldier, and to the church in your house:
Philemon 2

To the general assembly and church of the firstborn who are enrolled in heaven, and to God, the Judge of all, and to the spirits of the righteous made perfect,
Hebrews 12:23

As I mentioned earlier, the word "ekklēsia" appears over a hundred times in the New Testament. While most of the time it speaks of the people as the church, there seem to be two ways the Scripture speaks of the church in the New Testament.

The first way refers to the body of Christ as a whole. In the Bible, the body of Christ includes all of us who believe, regardless of time and space.

One example would be Hebrews 12:23 mentioning the general assembly and church of the firstborn who are enrolled in heaven.

The second way refers to a specific group of the people of the Lord as a church in whatever time and space they are. For example, we are told to tell the church if we have a brother who sins and refuses to listen in private first, then even with one or two witnesses. We know this passage cannot possibly refer to the church as the whole body of Christ, but the specific group we are with.

There are also many verses where a church is associated with the name of a certain city. There are also times where believers meeting in specific houses are called churches. Scripture also describes churches in several communities in different cities within a certain region.

Because of this second way the Scripture refers to the church, there are many different teachings and interpretations on what the church is and is not. Due to disagreements among believers, there have been many splits and divisions.

Some say there should be only one church (ekklēsia) in a city so all who believe and who live in that city must gather together in one place to be that church. It is true that there are many churches that are associated with city names in the New Testament. We see seven churches in Asia that represent seven cities in Revelation. Some might therefore conclude that there can be only one church in one city.

In the Old Testament as well, a city represented the people who lived in it and their ways. Sodom and Gomorrah were sinful cities in their times; therefore, God destroyed them both with brimstone and fire out of heaven. God sent Jonah to Nineveh and said that He had compassion on this great city where there were more than one hundred twenty thousand people who didn't know their right hand from their left. All those people were represented by the name of their city simply because that is the way God saw them. Our Lord Jesus rebuked cities where He had done many of His miracles such as Chorazin, Bethsaida, and Capernaum because of their unrepentance. Those cities represented the people and their heart conditions, ways of life, disobedience, and unrepentance.

Of course all believers in the Lord Jesus Christ live by the same life which comes from Christ, so if we look at one city, there can only be one church there according to spiritual nature. So in that sense, I would gladly agree there is only one church in one city under the name of our Lord Jesus Christ. But that does not mean that all believers who live in that city must only gather as one group every time. Rather, they are one because they are all in Christ and live in the same city. In recent years, however, what the Lord has been showing me continuously is that it is not one city, one church; but rather, one body, one church. When the Lord looks at all believers, He sees and calls us the church, the ekklēsia, as a mass. He can also see and call all believers in a certain city the ekklēsia of that city. But we cannot assume that one church in one city means all the believers there must always gather together as one group in order to be the church. If the Lord sees us as one church in one city, all who believe in that city would be included whether they are gathered in one place or in many places or not gathered at all. The spiritual reality is how God sees those in a certain city who are His by faith.

Let me give you an example. When we think of a large

15

family that lives in various parts of the country, we might associate them with the city they live in or are close by. Think of the Kim family in Memphis, or in Dallas, or in New York. We would call it the Kim family in Memphis or the Kim family in Dallas or New York. We would not have to speak of the Kim family on such and such a street in a certain city, state and zip code to identify that family. A family in a city would be sufficient in many cases. Even a large family with many children who live in different houses throughout the city could be described as the family by that name in that city. But that does not mean that the Kim family in a certain city all live in the same house. Even if that large family lives in multiple houses and in various places, they are one family with one father or ancestor.

But as it is, they desire a better country, that is, a heavenly one. Therefore God is not ashamed to be called their God; for He has prepared a city for them.
Hebrews 11:16

For here we do not have a lasting city, but we are seeking the city which is to come.
Hebrews 13:14

All believers are waiting for the holy city, the New

Jerusalem, that will come down out of heaven. Even now all believers are citizens of the one and only kingdom of God. We may indeed live in different cities because we are in different places physically, but all believers have the same citizenship which is in heaven. And one day soon, all of us will be gathered to live in that holy city, the New Jerusalem. Praise the Lord!

In the first century, the apostles followed the teaching of the Lord by working and walking by the Holy Spirit. They went out to preach the gospel wherever they felt the Spirit led. By doing so, they were able to devote themselves to establishing the body of Christ which is the church (ekklēsia). The Lord used these apostles as foundation stones of the New Jerusalem. Thus, they preached the gospel and the body of Christ was established.

They preached the gospel of the Lord Jesus Christ everywhere they were led by the Spirit. Then, the people who received the gospel started gathering together in each city. Due to such issues as distance, they gathered together in each city apart from the believers in another city. Aside from practical constraints, Paul said that Christians should not be divided into different groups just because some followed Paul and others followed Apollos.

Now I mean this, that each one of you is saying, "I am of Paul," and "I of Apollos," and "I of Cephas," and "I of Christ." Has Christ been divided? Paul was not crucified for you, was he? Or were you baptized in the name of Paul?

1 Corinthians 1:12-13

In these days, there are many denominations and non-denominations that claim the name of our Lord Jesus Christ. Because of certain doctrines held as their way of interpreting Scripture, churches have been divided numerous times. But Christ is not divided and none of our teachers, doctrines, denominations or non-denominations were crucified for us. We are one people of God through our Lord and Savior Jesus Christ.

Regarding this, the Lord has shown me that because all believers are united in one body of Christ which is the church (ekklēsia), all of us who believe are God's house, family, descendants, and His people. For those who believe, this fact does not and cannot change based on whether they gather with other believers in a certain city or not. For if you have been born again into the body of Christ by faith, then you are also in the church which is His body. Because the Lord calls the body of Christ His church and His church the body, the relationship formula between the two has to be equal. The body of Christ = the Church.

Those who are saved and born again by believing in the Lord Jesus Christ belong in Him and live by His life. The whole community of all saved, born-again believers is the body of Christ or the church (ekklēsia). It is all of God who resurrected the body of Christ as a spiritual body and raised up that spiritual body as the church.

Only God can open people's hearts and cause them to be saved by faith. The spiritual body of Christ is not a religious building or an organization where you can go and sign up to be a member. You can go to Christian gatherings or places called churches for decades and meet regularly with the most spiritual and godly people, but unless you are born again by faith into the body of Christ, you cannot be a part of the church (ekklēsia).

Conversely, even when we are in any dark place, even in the lion's den in a wicked city, if we have faith in our Lord Jesus Christ, we belong to His church. The Lord does not call buildings His church just because we go there to gather in His name. The Lord looks at all who live by His life and His Spirit as His church and calls us ekklēsia; the Lord calls us as My people, My citizens. Our Lord calls us the church whenever and wherever we are gathered together, but He also calls us the church even when we are not gathered. He speaks of us in this way because we are those who believe and live by His life. Praise the Lord Jesus Christ who saved us and gave us life in His spiritual body!

So then, why is this body of Christ which is the church so important? What is the purpose that God is trying to accomplish through the body of Christ? In answer to these questions, God showed me the one body and the one church (ekklēsia).

Chapter 3
One Body, One Church
(One Ekklēsia)

The Bible tells us that all those who were born again by faith were born into one new man and one body. Notwithstanding denominations, non-denominations, and other divisions, in Christ there is only oneness. Scripture tells us about that oneness:

There is one body and one Spirit, just as also you were called in one hope of your calling; one Lord, one faith, one baptism, one God and Father of all who is over all and through all and in all.

Ephesians 4:4-6

This verse makes it clear that all believers in Christ share in oneness. One body, one Spirit, one hope, one Lord, one faith, one baptism, and one God and Father of all. But this is not the only verse that affirms our oneness and unity in the body of Christ.

For just as we have many members in one body and all the members do not have the same function, so we, who are many, are one body in Christ, and individually members one of another.

Romans 12:4-5

Since there is one bread, we who are many are one body; for we all partake of the one bread.

1 Corinthians 10:17

For by one Spirit we were all baptized into one body, whether Jews or Greeks, whether slaves or free, and we were all made to drink of one Spirit.

1 Corinthians 12:13

Let the peace of Christ rule in your hearts, to which indeed you were

called in one body; and be thankful.
  Colossians 3:15

Why do you think God made only one body? If He had wanted to, He could have made us into many spiritual bodies. He could have said in the Scripture that there is one Spirit but many different bodies; however, He does not say that. He says there is one body whether Jews or Greeks, slaves or free, and we were all made to drink of one Spirit. There is only one body and one Spirit. God reveals the reason behind that one body in the book of Ephesians.

But now in Christ Jesus you who formerly were far off have been brought near by the blood of Christ. For He Himself is our peace, who made both groups into one and broke down the barrier of the dividing wall, by abolishing in His flesh the enmity, which is the Law of commandments contained in ordinances, so that in Himself He might make the two into one new man, thus establishing peace, and might reconcile them both in one body to God through the cross, by it having put to death the enmity. And He came and preached peace to you who were far away, and peace to those who were near; for through Him we both have our access in one Spirit to the Father. So then you are no longer strangers and aliens, but you are fellow citizens with the saints, and are of God's household, having been built on the foundation of the apostles and prophets, Christ Jesus

Himself being the corner stone, in whom the whole building, being fitted together, is growing into a holy temple in the Lord, in whom you also are being built together into a dwelling of God in the Spirit.
Ephesians 2:13-22

In the Old Testament people had to stay far away from the presence of a holy God because of their fallen and sinful nature. Even such a holy God, because of His great desire, made a way to dwell among the Israelites through His presence in the tabernacle (a huge moveable tent), but the Israelites did not dare enter the Holy of Holies (or Most Holy Place) in that tabernacle. Not only could they not enter the Holy of Holies where the presence of God dwelled; they could not even have a sneak peek through the veil (on penalty of death). Only the high priest of Israel could enter, and that but once a year on the Day of Atonement.

Jesus Christ has made a way for us to walk into the Holy of Holies. He has opened the door, through His own body, so that we could be in the presence of the holy God by His blood and His sacrifice, praise the Lord! And now those who believe in Christ are themselves that Holy of Holies in which God dwells through His Spirit.

Or do you not know that your body is a temple of the Holy Spirit who is in you, whom you have from God, and that you are not your own? For you have been bought with a price: therefore glorify God in your body.

1 Corinthians 6:19-20

In the original Greek, Paul here uses not the general word for temple "hieron," but a special word referring to the inner part of the temple "naos" consisting of the Holy Place and the Holy of Holies (the sanctuary). This means that your body is not the external temple as we would normally think of it, but the inner part, the dwelling place, the sanctuary, where the Spirit of God dwells.

Therefore, brethren, since we have confidence to enter the holy place by the blood of Jesus, by a new and living way which He inaugurated for us through the veil, that is, His flesh,

Hebrews 10:19-20

By His blood and sacrifice, the veil of the temple was torn from top to bottom. (It is remarkable that it was torn not from bottom to top but from top to bottom.) That is why the verse said the veil is his flesh. The sacrifice of Jesus Christ made it possible for us to do what was impossible, to touch what was untouchable, to approach what was unapproachable, to access the inaccessible, to find what was hidden from us, all by the power and might of our holy God.

And Jesus cried out again with a loud voice, and yielded up His spirit. And behold, the veil of the temple was torn in two from top to bottom.

Matthew 27:50-51

This is how we who were enemies of God were able to draw near to Him and therefore to each other. Through His blood and sacrifice, our Lord Jesus Christ made us into one people, one body together reconciled to God.

Because of this, when God sees those who are in the body of Christ, He sees us through Christ who is our Head. We would never have had peace with a holy God except through the sacrifice of Christ's body, who was righteous, perfect, and blameless. Through Him, God has torn the veil and opened the way into the Holy of Holies that we might live in Christ Jesus as members of His body. Christ is the one and only Savior of His spiritual body which is the church (ekklēsia).

For the husband is the head of the wife, as Christ also is the head of

the church, He Himself being the Savior of the body.
Ephesians 5:23

There is therefore no wall between believers in Christ—not only between Jews and Gentiles but also between man and woman, young and old. He overcame all discrimination by making us into one body, the body of Christ. Christ reconciled all of us in one body to God through the cross and has put to death the enmity, once and for all.

For it was the Father's good pleasure for all the fullness to dwell in Him, and through Him to reconcile all things to Himself, having made peace through the blood of His cross; through Him, I say, whether things on earth or things in heaven.
And although you were formerly alienated and hostile in mind, engaged in evil deeds, yet He has now reconciled you in His fleshly body through death, in order to present you before Him holy and blameless and beyond reproach— if indeed you continue in the faith firmly established and steadfast, and not moved away from the hope of the gospel that you have heard, which was proclaimed in all creation under heaven, and of which I, Paul, was made a minister.
Colossians 1:19-23

This is the oneness, the one new man, the one body of

Christ, and the one church (ekklēsia) that was established and raised up through Christ. Think about it: if we can see that even Jews and Gentiles became one through the body of Christ, as different from one another as they were, how can we think that some believers are in the body with us and some are not, if we all believe in the name of our Lord Jesus Christ? Of course, the Scripture makes clear that there are those who are preaching another Jesus, a different spirit, and a different gospel. We ought to be led by the Holy Spirit, abide in the word of God, and stand firm to discern, reprove, rebuke, and exhort one another to press on toward the goal in Christ Jesus. Here I am talking about all faithful believers who put their hope in Christ Jesus alone. If we do this, there should be no division among those who are together in the body of Christ.

Do not lie to one another, since you laid aside the old self with its evil practices, and have put on the new self who is being renewed to a true knowledge according to the image of the One who created him— a renewal in which there is no distinction between Greek and Jew, circumcised and uncircumcised, barbarian, Scythian, slave and freeman, but Christ is all, and in all.

Colossians 3:9-11

I do not want you to be unaware, brethren, that often I have planned to come to you (and have been prevented so far) so that I may obtain some fruit among you also, even as among the rest of the Gentiles. I am under obligation both to Greeks and to barbarians, both to the wise and to the foolish.

Romans 1:13-14

If there is no distinction between Greek and Jew, circumcised and uncircumcised, Barbarian, Scythian, slave and freeman, the wise and the foolish, I can confidently say that there are also no Americans, Koreans, Swedes, Asians, Africans, or Europeans in His body, but rather Christ is all, and in all.

Then what is God doing with this one body, the body of Christ?

Chapter 4
What God is Doing with One Body

In a typical city in the United States, it isn't hard to find many churches with different signs describing their denominations and non-denominations. Most people don't even know what all the denominations mean and where they came from. However, based on the Scriptures we have already examined, we should be able to see that where people go on Sundays often has little to do with being in the body of Christ.

Let me give you an example. Suppose you are invited into someone's family every Sunday to have a meal and spend time with them. You might begin to be more like them in the way you think, act, or believe. You might even begin to feel like a part of that family since you are so close to them. But in reality, you are not part of that family. No matter how often you visit or how close you are to them, you do not become a part of that family because you show up there every Sunday. Apart from becoming an "in law" by marriage, you can only become a part of someone's family by being born or adopted into that family.

Let me give you another example. You can go on the campus of a certain college every day and even sit in their classrooms. If no one stops you, you might even manage to sit through an entire course. You could learn some of what they teach in those classrooms. But unless you are actually enrolled in that college, you are not considered a student, and you will not get a diploma by just showing up and attending classes.

Do you see my point? The body of Christ, which is the church (ekklēsia), is not a social club or a membership-based organization where you can just show up or sign up. It is not a place where you can be a part by having a commitment to attend and do good for others. It is not merely a place where people come to be healed or to heal. Neither is it a physical location where you can choose to go or not go.

The body of Christ is the mass of born-again believers in Christ. Christ has brought all of us by the power of the gospel, which is the power of God, into His own spiritual body. Therefore, we cannot become a part of that spiritual body of Christ by going to physical buildings or meeting places; we can only become a part by being born again, by believing in our heart on the Lord Jesus Christ. By faith, we are made into that one body of Christ which is the church (ekklēsia). May we all clearly see that spiritual body regardless of whenever or wherever we live. I so long for all of us to see the body of Christ which is the church (ekklēsia) stretching across the nations, cultures, denominations and non-denominations, generations, and ages.

After these things I looked, and behold, a great multitude which no one could count, from every nation and all tribes and peoples and tongues, standing before the throne and before the Lamb, clothed in white robes, and palm branches were in their hands; and they cry out with a loud voice, saying,

"Salvation to our God who sits on the throne, and to the Lamb."
Revelation 7:9-10

Once we grasp the reality of the ekklēsia, which is all believers in Christ, we will then be curious to know what God's purpose for this one body of Christ might be.

From whom the whole body, being fitted and held together by what every joint supplies, according to the proper working of each individual part, causes the growth of the body for the building up of itself in love.
Ephesians 4:16

Paul mentions this again in the book of Colossians.

And not holding fast to the head, from whom the entire body, being supplied and held together by the joints and ligaments, grows with a growth which is from God.
Colossians 2:19

The books of Ephesians and Colossians have many similarities. In both letters, Paul puts much emphasis on what the church (ekklēsia) is and what God is intending to do with the church. Interestingly, Paul explains the same concept in somewhat different ways. In Ephesians, Paul says the growth of the body is for "the building up of itself in love," but in Colossians he says it "grows with a growth which is from God."

We know these passages both speak of that one body of Christ, so these explanations do not contradict, but rather complement, one another. Together they give a fuller explanation of the growth of one and the same body. We can see this in what Paul wrote to the Corinthians.

I planted, Apollos watered, but God was causing the growth. So then neither the one who plants nor the one who waters is anything, but God who causes the growth. Now he who plants and he who waters are one; but each will receive his own reward according to his own labor.

1 Corinthians 3:6-8

In this passage, Paul is talking about Apollos's work and his own work in Corinth. He indicates that his work was like planting and Apollos's work like watering. Thus, Paul could have said that both he and Apollos made the saints in Corinth grow in the Lord. But he goes on to say that neither the one who plants nor the one who waters is anything, but it is God who causes the growth. Paul also said he who plants and he who waters are one. Does that mean Paul and Apollos are one and the same person? Of course not. It is God who worked through both Paul and Apollos. Both the planting and the watering were God's work. God is, however, going to reward Paul and Apollos according to their individual labor. The bottom line is that they were both used by God in the work He had purposed.

Brothers and sisters, do you see that the body of Christ

was being built up in love through Paul and Apollos? And do you see that it was all from God who caused the work and growth? God not only dwells in us, but He also works through us to grow and build up His body in love. That is why Paul said that Apollos and he were not anything but servants who did what the Lord gave them to do.

Now I rejoice in my sufferings for your sake, and in my flesh I do my share on behalf of His body, which is the church, in filling up what is lacking in Christ's afflictions. Of this church I was made a minister according to the stewardship from God bestowed on me for your benefit, so that I might fully carry out the preaching of the word of God,
    Colossians 1:24-25

In the letter to the Colossians, we see clearly what servants of Christ like Paul were working for. Christ's servants are to suffer for one another's sake on behalf of His body, which is the church, in filling up what is lacking in Christ's afflictions. Let's consider this last phrase. How can anything be lacking in Christ afflictions when He paid it all and announced that it is finished?

Yes, Jesus finished all. But now He is working through us His body and letting us participate. It is God's work in us that was lacking in Christ's afflictions. He not only brings us into His spiritual body, but also gives us opportunity to participate in what He is doing. It is not because God needs us, but He wants and desires us to be fellow workers with Him. Hallelujah!

For we are God's fellow workers; you are God's field, God's building.
   1 Corinthians 3:9

And we sent Timothy, our brother and God's fellow worker in the gospel of Christ, to strengthen and encourage you as to your faith,
   1 Thessalonians 3:2

For it is God who is at work in you, both to will and to work for His good pleasure.
   Philippians 2:13

Now the God of peace, who brought up from the dead the great Shepherd of the sheep through the blood of the eternal covenant, even Jesus our Lord, equip you in every good thing to do His will, working in us that which is pleasing in His sight, through Jesus Christ, to whom be the glory forever and ever. Amen.
   Hebrews 13:20-21

In the letter to the Philippians, it says God is at work in you to will and to work for His good pleasure. I pray that God would show you His good pleasure which works in you to will and to work to make you a participant in His work.

But someone may ask, can God use just anyone? Or can He only use people like Paul and Apollos? Who does God use these days? Let us look to the Scripture for answers.

And He gave some as apostles, and some as prophets, and some as evangelists, and some as pastors and teachers, for the equipping of the saints for the work of service, to the building up of the body of Christ; until we all attain to the unity of the faith, and of the knowledge of the Son of God, to a mature man, to the measure of the stature which belongs to the fullness of Christ.

Ephesians 4:11-13

Here we see that God has gifted certain people to be apostles, prophets, evangelists, pastors, and teachers. Each is given a measure of grace so that they can carry out such work. If you only read verse 11, you may think that since you are not one of these, you cannot participate in what God is doing. But is it true that only apostles, prophets, evangelists, pastors, and teachers are able to work for the body of Christ? Absolutely not. The clear role and purpose of these gifted people is found in the following verse 12.

He says that these people are supposed to be

equipping the saints for the work of service, to the building up of the body of Christ. Let me say it again, these gifted people are given their gifts to equip the other saints so that they can do God's work and build up the body of Christ. Their job is to enable the other members of Christ's body to serve one another in love so that the growth and upbuilding of the body can happen! And of course it won't be the saints alone who will cause this growth, but God, who dwells inside of them, will cause them to work so as to bring about the growth that comes from Him!

I would like to emphasize one other thing in this passage: the Greek word for service is "diakonia." Some may misunderstand "the work of service" as some small, insignificant volunteer work one might find to do. That is not true. This word "diakonia" is also translated in the Bible as ministry. This work of service was pursued by both apostles and disciples. When Paul and Barnabas were on their missionary journeys, it is said that they were engaging in ministry. The Greek word used there was also "diakonia." My point is that the work of service is not some small, insignificant work set out for ordinary saints, but rather that there is simply no limit to what that work of service can be. No one should feel that they are "just ordinary" saints since there is no such thing as an ordinary saint. Every Christian is being trained to be a "minister" (servant) in the biblical sense of the word.

Here is another point of clarification: when the Bible

uses the word ministry or minister, it does not refer to someone qualified and educated to have a ministry or to be a minister. Over time, the English word "ministry" came to describe some special and reputable work. A minister came to mean a member of the clergy or head of a government department who was appointed after obtaining appropriate qualifications, training or education. These are not the meanings of these words in the Bible. Indeed, it was quite the contrary. Ministry (diakonia) meant service and minister (diakonos) meant servant or attendant. Among the ones who were called ministers (diakonos) were Paul, Apollos, Timothy, Phoebe, Tychicus, other disciples, and even Jesus Christ. These words "minister" and "ministry" did not mean highly esteemed. They meant those who took a lowly place to serve others as Christ did.

But the greatest among you shall be your servant (diakonos).
Matthew 23:11

Sitting down, He called the twelve and said to them, "If anyone wants to be first, he shall be last of all and servant (diakonos) of all."
Mark 9:35

It's clear that anyone who has a heart for the Lord Jesus Christ can become a minister and have a ministry simply by being a servant and being of service to others. If we serve the Lord with a willing heart, we are already His ministers and servants (diakonos), and we already have a ministry and a service (diakonia) for His good pleasure.

Brothers and sisters, the body of Christ does not grow only through the few people who are apostles, prophets, evangelists, pastors, or teachers. In the body of Christ, to which we all belong, we must be equipped and ready for our own individual works of service to one another in love, thus causing growth in one other. And you can see the result of saints being equipped and ready in the next verses of Ephesians 4. Praise the Lord who is working in and through us to enable us to participate in His glorious work!

As a result, we are no longer to be children, tossed here and there by waves and carried about by every wind of doctrine, by the trickery of men, by craftiness in deceitful scheming; but speaking the truth in love, we are to grow up in all aspects into Him who is the head, even Christ, from whom the whole body, being fitted and held together by what every joint supplies, according to the proper working of each individual part, causes the growth of the body for the building up of itself in love.
Ephesians 4:14-16

These verses show us how God is growing the spiritual body of Christ through all born-again believers. He called us to be born again for Him in order to work through us and cause the growth and building up of His one, spiritual, living body. Thus, Jesus Christ's salvation of mankind is not just for the purpose of individuals being saved, but also for the ultimate purpose of bringing us together as Christ's body and enabling us to participate in His work, which is to cause this growth and building up in love so that all things might be summed up in Christ.

When does this spiritual body of Christ which is the church (ekklēsia) become full grown or complete, and what purpose does God accomplish through this body of Christ? To understand more of His purpose behind all this work, God led me to the Old Testament to show me what it is all for and why He started what He started.

Chapter 5
What Is It All For?

Matthew 6:21 says, "For where your treasure is, there your heart will be also." Jesus was telling us not to store up treasures on earth, but in heaven, and He made it clear that wherever our treasure is kept, that is where our heart is kept as well. Obviously, this was spoken for us and for our sake. But where is God's treasure and where is His heart? As I was considering this passage one day, I felt God's heart. I felt that God's heart has always been with His people. As

God created all things in the heavens and on the earth, He has always been treasuring His people on earth. That is why, all through history, His heart has been with His people. And we know that God is love.

So this love of God has been with His people all along. Even now, more than ever, this love of God is with His people, not only with His people in this present generation but also with the entire body of Christ, spanning the ages, which is the church, for the building up of itself in love and the summing up of all things in Christ. Isn't that amazing? God created all things in the heavens and on the earth with the intention that His amazing love would sum up all things in Christ. Furthermore, He made us a part of that amazing purpose. Think about that! God not only created us as a part of His creation, but also, through the sacrifice of His one and only begotten Son, He is enabling and allowing us to participate in His own purpose because of His love. Praise the Lord God Almighty! The Gospel of John speaks plainly of that love:

"For God so loved the world, that He gave His only begotten Son, that whoever believes in Him shall not perish, but have eternal life. For God did not send the Son into the world to judge the world, but that the world might be saved through Him."
John 3:16-17

God had the same heart in the Old Testament that desired to bring His people together and to let them participate in His work. This is evident in the building of the tabernacle where God dwelled. As we look at the Scripture, let us be reminded of the ways of the Lord, for He desires the same participation from us today.

"Tell the sons of Israel to raise a contribution for Me; from every man whose heart moves him you shall raise My contribution."
Exodus 25:2

"Let them construct a sanctuary for Me, that I may dwell among them."
Exodus 25:8

Did you see that God gave the Israelites an opportunity to contribute to His work? God did not say to have wealthy people or gifted people contribute, but He said every man whose heart moved him should raise the contribution. These are the same people who, even after He brought them out of Egypt, complained and grumbled against Him, yet He still desired to dwell among them.

Also, please note that when we hear the word "contribution" we usually think of giving our money. But here I am speaking much more broadly of utilizing our spiritual gifts to build up the body of Christ, of bringing freewill offerings of our time and talents and ultimately ourselves to the Lord's work. Let us remember that the building work for the body of Christ is being done with spiritual things and not with material things.

Everyone whose heart stirred him and everyone whose spirit moved him came and brought the LORD'S contribution for the work of the tent of meeting and for all its service and for the holy garments. Then all whose hearts moved them, both men and women, came and brought brooches and earrings and signet rings and bracelets, all articles of gold; so did every man who presented an offering of gold to the LORD. Every man, who had in his possession blue and purple and scarlet material and fine linen and goats' hair and rams' skins dyed red and porpoise skins, brought them. Everyone who could make a contribution of silver and bronze brought the LORD'S contribution; and every man who had in his possession acacia wood for any work of the service brought it. All the skilled women spun with their hands, and brought what they had spun, in blue and purple and scarlet material and in fine linen. All the women whose heart stirred with a skill spun the goats' hair. The rulers brought the onyx stones and the stones for setting for the ephod and for the breastpiece; and the spice and the oil for the light and for the anointing oil and for the fragrant incense. The Israelites, all the men and women, whose heart moved them to bring material for all the work, which the LORD had commanded through Moses to be done, brought a freewill offering to the LORD.

Exodus 35:21-29

In Exodus 35, it is said that everyone whose heart stirred him and everyone whose spirit moved him came and brought the Lord's contribution for the work. Again, it wasn't by selection, training, wealth, or education, but by their hearts that they were able to bring freewill offerings to the Lord.

And they said to Moses, "The people are bringing much more than enough for the construction work which the LORD commanded us to perform." So Moses issued a command, and a proclamation was circulated throughout the camp, saying, "Let no man or woman any longer perform work for the contributions of the sanctuary." Thus the people were restrained from bringing any more. For the material they had was sufficient and more than enough for all the work, to perform it.

Exodus 36:5-7

Consider these verses. They tell us that the Israelites brought much more than enough for the work. What an honor and privilege it is to be able to participate in the building of God's dwelling place! It was such a blessing for the Israelites to have willing hearts in bringing their contributions. But do you think God needed something from the Israelites to build Himself a dwelling place? What would God need? It is He who created all and who is all-powerful and all-knowing. It was He who brought the Israelites out of Egypt by performing great miracles and signs, then fed and kept them for forty years in the wilderness providing their every need.

It is not that God needed the Israelites to bring Him contributions, but that God wanted His people to participate in what He was doing. And did God only allow them to bring contributions, but then did the work Himself? No, He did everything through people even though it was He who caused everything to be done.

Then Moses said to the sons of Israel, "See, the LORD has called by name Bezalel the son of Uri, the son of Hur, of the tribe of Judah. And He has filled him with the Spirit of God, in wisdom, in understanding and in knowledge and in all craftsmanship; to make designs for working in gold and in silver and in bronze, and in the cutting of stones for settings and in the carving of wood, so as to perform in every inventive work. He also has put in his heart to teach, both he and Oholiab, the son of Ahisamach, of the tribe of Dan. He has filled them with skill to perform every work of an engraver and of a designer and of an embroiderer, in blue and in purple and in scarlet material, and in fine linen, and of a weaver, as performers of every work and makers of designs.

Exodus 35:30-35

Do you see here that God called Bezalel and filled him with His Spirit, in wisdom, in understanding, and in knowledge and in all craftsmanship? Is it Bezalel who had the wisdom, understanding, knowledge, and craftsmanship to do all the work he did? No, it says clearly that God filled him with the Spirit of God to enable and to equip him. Do you remember what I said earlier about Paul and Apollos? Neither Paul who planted nor Apollos who watered were anything because it was God who caused the growth. God worked through Paul and Apollos so that they could participate in His work and He could reward them.

To return to Exodus, it says that God also put it in Bezalel's heart to teach, both he and Oholiab, and filled them with skill to perform every work. So He didn't just enable them to do the work, He also put in them a heart to teach. Can you see that God planned and carried out all the details and also gave the way of reproducing His work through teaching, through passing it on? For the rest of the story, take the time to read Exodus 25-40.

Some may find those chapters difficult because of all the detail but read them and consider whether it was the skillful people who carried out all those details or was it God who commanded and worked through people to construct His sanctuary.

The Bible does not preserve all these details just because they are historical facts. They are recorded to show that God planned, directed, guided, and worked through all these processes. It was His desire that the children of Israel participate in His work. And because of the same desire God has for us, He has predestined us and called us in like fashion to participate in what He is doing. You can see this clearly in Romans 8.

And we know that God causes all things to work together for good to those who love God, to those who are called according to His purpose. For those whom He foreknew, He also predestined to become conformed to the image of His Son, so that He would be the firstborn among many brethren; and these whom He predestined, He also called; and these whom He called, He also justified; and these whom He justified, He also glorified.
Romans 8:28-30

These verses are some of the most popular and frequently quoted verses in the Bible. I myself have them memorized and have quoted them frequently. But when we quote these verses, we usually quote only the first part: "we know that God causes all things to work together for good to those who love God."

I asked God who we are and what we are about and

what is the purpose of our being the body of Christ, and He showed me these verses. I realized that I had often quoted, but not deeply understood, the latter part of these verses, which refers to those who are called according to His purpose, whom He foreknew, predestined, called, justified, and glorified. The Lord showed me that these are the processes He is taking us through in order to enable us to participate in His work. He did not call us just so that we can benefit from all things working together. He called us according to HIS PURPOSE. In other words, because God had a will and a purpose, He foreknew us before the creation, He predestined us to become conformed to the image of His Son, and at the predetermined time He called us in order to justify and to glorify us.

Then the cloud covered the tent of meeting, and the glory of the LORD filled the tabernacle. Moses was not able to enter the tent of meeting because the cloud had settled on it, and the glory of the LORD filled the tabernacle.

Exodus 40:34-35

Look at the glory of the LORD. Even Moses was not able to enter into the tent of meeting because the glory of the Lord filled the tabernacle. This is the glory of our God. No one can dare touch the glory of the Lord. And the glory of the Lord can fill everything at any time.

Brothers and sisters, do you see, in these last days, that God has enabled and allowed us to participate in this process of filling up all things with His glory through Christ? Praise the Lord! Even in this very moment as I am writing this, my heart is so moved and stirred, that I have had to stop and praise the Lord. But this is not all there is. Our corporate purpose is not to build a dwelling place for God, for already Jesus Christ Himself has established such a dwelling place once for all with His own body.

Then comes the end, when He hands over the kingdom to the God and Father, when He has abolished all rule and all authority and power. For He must reign until He has put all His enemies under His feet. The last enemy that will be abolished is death. For He has put all things in subjection under His feet. But when He says, "All things are put in subjection," it is evident that He is excepted who put all things in subjection to Him. When all things are subjected to Him, then the Son Himself also will be subjected to the One who subjected all things to Him, so that God may be all in all.

1 Corinthians 15:24-28

This is the corporate purpose for all of us who are members of the body of Christ. God does not want us just to enter into eternity with Him. He wants us also to be partakers in His work and joined with Him in HIS PURPOSE.

Christ was faithful as a Son over His house—whose house we are, if we hold fast our confidence and the boast of our hope firm until the end.

Hebrews 3:6

For we have become partakers of Christ, if we hold fast the beginning of our assurance firm until the end,

Hebrews 3:14

Chapter 6
The Summing up of
All Things in Jesus Christ

I began this book by talking about the church (ekklēsia) and how it is another name for the body of Christ. I started there because I am writing this letter to my fellow members of the body of Christ, those who are believers in Christ. If I were writing a letter to the lost world, I would not start with a definition of what the church is. Instead I would begin by telling of the true and living God and His Son, Jesus Christ. For without knowing God the Father and

God the Son, there is nothing to begin with.

We have many religions in our world today. Some recognize a deity somewhat like the God of the Bible. But the major difference is that we believe in the Son of God, Jesus Christ as our Savior, God, King, Lord, Shepherd, Guardian, Bridegroom, and everything, as He is our all in all. If Jesus Christ is the center of our life and our lives depend on Him as the source of all life, hope, peace, joy, and everything else, then we have much to fellowship about. However, Jesus Christ is not the center of some peoples' lives. They don't worship or serve Him, and so with them we must begin by sharing the gospel.

The reason is very simple. Without Jesus Christ, we cannot get to God. Without Jesus Christ, we do not have the presence of God in our lives. Without Jesus Christ, we would be still condemned in our sin. Without Jesus Christ, we would have nothing. Without Jesus, God's intention and purpose make no sense. Jesus Christ is the center of everything, the Alpha and the Omega, the First and the Last, the beginning and the end.

Since we are all believers in Christ, hopefully we all know the stories of the Old Testament. The events from creation to the time of Jesus are recorded in the Old Testament. Other than roughly four hundred years in between the Old and New Testaments (after Malachi), the Bible is divided before and after Christ's time on earth as the Old and the New Testaments. When I became a new

Christian, a newborn baby in Christ, I thought of the Old Testament as just old stories, mostly long and boring. Then one day, God started to show me His ways through the Old Testament. God spoke to me through the lives of people in the Old Testament, showing me how He carried, delivered, cared for, worked in, and did many wondrous things with them. Then He showed me that He is doing all of that with me as well. It was when God showed me that I am on the same journey as the Israelites that I started paying more attention to those Old Testament stories.

When I was reading and searching the heart of God in the Old Testament, one specific theme impressed me: God's faithfulness to His people. Ever since the fall of mankind, God's pursuit of His people was relentless throughout the stories of the Old Testament. Not only did God pursue His people Israel, but He also made covenants with them to turn them from their sins and wicked ways. He was even willing to come and dwell in the tabernacle (a moveable, tent-like structure) to be among His people. The God of the universe, the creator of all things, the Almighty, dwelt in a tent to be with His people. That is beyond imagination! I know God had to construct that elaborate dwelling place because He is Holy. Because He is Holy, He dwelt among His people behind layers of separation since they were defiled and fallen in their evil nature. But even so, God's heart was after His people. In spite of their sin, it was His desire to be with them. That is why special arrangements such as covenants, the tabernacle, and the temple were necessary. God's heart, His desire for a more permanent place among His people, was not known until David, a man after God's own heart. Because of his bloodshed, however, even King David was not fit to build a more permanent structure where God could dwell among His people. But because David was after the heart of God and found favor in God's sight, he was blessed to make preparations for that temple which Solomon, his son, built, so that God might finally have a house among His people.

I always looked up to David as a man after God's own heart and having the desire to build a dwelling place for God. While I still thank God for the testimony of David, I now know that God had a higher goal than dwelling temporarily in a house made by human hands. While people naturally desire to worship God in buildings, temples, houses, or other structures men may build, God does not dwell in such places. Stephen in Acts 7 made it plain:

David found favor in God's sight, and asked that he might find a dwelling place for the God of Jacob. But it was Solomon who built a house for Him. However, the Most High does not dwell in houses made by human hands; as the prophet says:

'Heaven is My throne, And earth is the footstool of My feet; What kind of house will you build for Me?' says the Lord, 'Or what place is there for My repose? Was it not My hand which made all these things?'
Acts 7:46-50

If I had read only the Old Testament, it would seem to me that God's pursuit of His people and His finding a dwelling place among them was impossible. Even with God's efforts at turning Israel around so many times with promises, warnings, and covenants, human beings just could not keep up their end of the bargain. The Old Testament is full of the struggles God had with His people.

Even after building Solomon's temple, we see that the Israelites again forsook God, burned incense to other gods, sacrificed to idols, and did many evils in the sight of God. Finally, He sent them into Babylonian captivity and Jerusalem was burned down by king Nebuchadnezzar of Babylon. In view of the struggles God had with the Israelites, it is clear that there was no human solution for God's "dilemma." I see the overarching message of the Old Testament as God's faithfulness to His people in His ongoing efforts to dwell with them in a permanent way.

This heartbreaking situation demanded an ultimate solution. God's longing to be with His people, yet His people being defiled, unholy, and evil in nature, the continuing struggle to make some arrangement work, God's never-ending pursuit of His people—all these pointed to the need for an answer that only God could bring. Everything in the Old Testament existed to prove the need for something greater and truly permanent, something beyond the temporary arrangements God had with His people. There had to be something to cover the iniquity of human nature once and for all, something to bring back and restore the relationship God had intended and desired even before creation.

And we all know what happened. Jesus Christ happened. So now we have insight into the fulfillment and restoration plan of God. His Son Jesus Christ is the ultimate sacrifice and the ultimate solution. Jesus Christ was the complete fix for God's dilemma with His people. He, the Son of God, came in human flesh as the Son of Man and replaced the temple that took forty-six years to build and raised it in three days. Let me repeat this amazing and most important event ever in history: Jesus Christ came as the obedient Son of God and sacrificed His body to be the solution to God's dilemma of desiring to dwell with His people who weren't holy. Now His people could be sanctified through the offering of the body of Jesus once and for all, and God is now able to dwell with His people. Praise the Lord Jesus Christ!

Then He said, "Behold, I have come to do Your will." He takes away the first in order to establish the second. By this will we have been sanctified through the offering of the body of Jesus Christ once for all.

Hebrews 10:9-10

This sacrifice of Jesus Christ fulfilled the Scripture. That is exactly why every story, every prophecy, every great man of God in the Old Testament is a foreshadowing or picture of Jesus Christ coming to accomplish and fulfill what God's heart has always been after: to dwell with His people and to have a relationship with His people.

After this, Jesus, knowing that all things had already been accomplished, to fulfill the Scripture, said, "I am thirsty." A jar full of sour wine was standing there; so they put a sponge full of the sour wine upon a branch of hyssop and brought it up to His mouth. Therefore when Jesus had received the sour wine, He said, "It is finished!" And He bowed His head and gave up His spirit.

John 19:28-30

It is significant that in Matthew's parallel account, rather than saying He "gave up," it says He "yielded up"

His spirit. It wasn't that Jesus gave up His spirit as one might surrender out of a sense of exhaustion or defeat, but that He deliberately yielded up His spirit for the will of God. Here we have the sacrifice of the one and only obedient Son that God ever had.

When Jesus Christ was on the cross, it appeared to be mankind's darkest hour. For God's enemy Satan, it probably seemed to him his most victorious moment. But praise the Lord God Almighty, we know Jesus didn't stay in the tomb but gloriously rose from the dead! Our Lord Jesus Christ was resurrected by the mighty power of God, and not only Jesus, but also all who believe in Him are risen with Him.

So the mystery of God's will that all things be summed up in Christ has been revealed and is being accomplished even today.

He made known to us the mystery of His will, according to His kind intention which He purposed in Him with a view to an administration suitable to the fullness of the times, that is, the summing up of all things in Christ, things in the heavens and things on the earth.
Ephesians 1:9-10

Here Paul explains why God created all things in the heavens and on the earth: through his amazing love, God's heart was to gather all things together that they might be summed up in Christ, things in the heavens and things on the earth. To gather up all things in Christ, Christ's physical body was planted in the earth through death and was resurrected a spiritual body.

It is only through Christ's spiritual body that all things can be summed up together for eternity. Because we were born on the earth with physical and mortal bodies, we were not made eternal. But by being born again into the body of Christ, we have become eternally alive in Him. And this body of Christ, which is His church (ekklēsia), is being made ready as His bride, His new Jerusalem, and His dwelling place—His everything being summed up in Christ.

Chapter 7
The Wedding of the Bridegroom and the Bride

If you are married, I am sure you remember the day of your wedding and how hard it was for you to wait because you longed for that day so much. Do you remember the joy of becoming one with your loved one after such a long wait? Do you remember the time when you were preparing and dressing for the wedding with such joy and excitement? Even if you have not been married, you know that a wedding day is full of joy and excitement for the bridegroom and the bride.

God made man and woman to love each another. And because of that love, they enter into the commitment of marriage. The two become one. I believe God created this natural process of marriage in anticipation of His purpose for the body of Christ.

When a man or a woman find another that they love, they desire to enter into a committed relationship. Having Been committed to join each other in marriage by being engaged, afterwards they become a bridegroom and a bride. As soon as they have set their wedding date, both bridegroom and bride look forward with great excitement to the coming of that day. Their desire for one another is very clearly seen and expressed in the wedding itself. Think of the moment when the bride enters and walks towards the bridegroom. Everyone's eyes first turn to see the bride, who has been perfectly prepared and ready, then they will turn to the bridegroom to see the joyful excitement on his face. When the bridegroom first sees his bride walk through the door, beautifully prepared for the wedding, his eyes light up and his face expresses how happy he is. The bridegroom and bride's first sight of each other is to me the most exciting moment of the wedding, because it says that their long wait is over and they are now in the presence of one another as the two of them become one.

This is the purpose of the body of Christ. It is God's good will for a man and a woman to have love and longing for one another until the wedding day brings them together. And as they become one, they set out on a life of joy and happiness together "for as long as they both shall live."

This relationship is not something God only introduces in the New Testament. It is no surprise that He prefigures it in His relationship with Israel in the Old Testament.

"It will come about in that day," declares the LORD,
"That you will call Me Ishi
And will no longer call Me Baali.
Hosea 2:16

Here the word "ishi" means man or husband, and "Baali" means "my master." It can be translated as:

That you will call Me my husband
And will no longer call Me my master.

In this passage God is showing His intention of changing His relationship with Israel from being Israel's master to being Israel's husband, something deeper. As you read more in Hosea 2, you can see His intentions.

"I will betroth you to Me forever;
Yes, I will betroth you to Me in righteousness and in justice,
In lovingkindness and in compassion,
And I will betroth you to Me in faithfulness.
Then you will know the LORD.
Hosea 2:19-20

This is expressed in other places in the Old Testament also.

'Return, O faithless sons,' declares the LORD;
'For I am a master to you,
And I will take you one from a city and two from a family,
And I will bring you to Zion.'
Jeremiah 3:14

In some translations the above phrase *"For I am a master to you"* is translated as *"For I am married to you."* This is because the Hebrew word "ba`al," which is translated as "master" here, also has the meaning of being married to a husband rather than just being mastered or ruled over. You can also see the concept of God being a husband to his bride Israel in the first and eighth verses of this chapter.

God says, "If a husband divorces his wife
And she goes from him
And belongs to another man,
Will he still return to her?
Will not that land be completely polluted?
But you are a harlot with many lovers;
Yet you turn to Me," declares the LORD.
Jeremiah 3:1

And I saw that for all the adulteries of faithless Israel, I had sent her
away and given her a writ of divorce, yet her treacherous sister Judah
did not fear; but she went and was a harlot also.
Jeremiah 3:8

There are many Scriptures where God expresses His love not only as the Maker but also as the Husband who loves Israel.

"For your husband is your Maker,
Whose name is the LORD of hosts;
And your Redeemer is the Holy One of Israel,
Who is called the God of all the earth.
Isaiah 54:5

For as a young man marries a virgin,
So your sons will marry you;
And as the bridegroom rejoices over the bride,
So your God will rejoice over you.
Isaiah 62:5

We know that this marriage or betrothal was never fully realized in the Old Testament. When Jesus came to fulfill the Scriptures, this relationship was also fulfilled. Here is how John the Baptist described his past as Jesus's "best man."

He who has the bride is the bridegroom; but the friend of the bridegroom, who stands and hears him, rejoices greatly because of the bridegroom's voice. So this joy of mine has been made full. He must increase, but I must decrease.
John 3:29

Jesus also spoke of this relationship.

And Jesus said to them, "The attendants of the bridegroom cannot mourn as long as the bridegroom is with them, can they? But the days will come when the bridegroom is taken away from them, and then

they will fast.
  Matthew 9:15

God spoke of a new covenant in Jeremiah, and Jesus fulfilled that covenant with His people. Let's look at the covenant Jeremiah spoke of.

"Behold, days are coming," declares the LORD, *"when I will make a new covenant with the house of Israel and with the house of Judah, not like the covenant which I made with their fathers in the day I took them by the hand to bring them out of the land of Egypt, My covenant which they broke, although I was a husband to them," declares the* LORD. *"But this is the covenant which I will make with the house of Israel after those days," declares the* LORD, *"I will put My law within them and on their heart I will write it; and I will be their God, and they shall be My people. They will not teach again, each man his neighbor and each man his brother, saying, 'Know the* LORD,' *for they will all know Me, from the least of them to the greatest of them," declares the* LORD, *"for I will forgive their iniquity, and their sin I will remember no more."*
  Jeremiah 31:31-34

This is the exact covenant Jesus spoke of in the New Testament.

For this is My blood of the covenant, which is poured out for many for forgiveness of sins.
Matthew 26:28

Let me add something that has helped me understand what Jesus did in making this covenant. We all know that in His new covenant He saved us with His own blood, that He is our Savior because He died and came to life again to rescue us. But how do we know that Jesus also fulfilled that role of bridegroom and husband? It is clearly taught in such New Testament books as Ephesians and Revelation. There is also historical information that sheds light on this subject.

When I was looking into this question, I was directed to the culture and time in which Jesus lived. As I considered these ancient wedding and marriage customs, I was able to see that what Jesus did perfectly demonstrated that He is indeed our bridegroom.

In the Jewish culture of that day, in order for a man to be betrothed (engaged), he had to come to a written agreement with the father of the woman. It was more than a modern-day engagement. It involved a legal contract process called "erusin." Along with signing a legal document, the man had to give a gift to "purchase" the bride. And since it was a binding contract (like a formal covenant), after the betrothal, the man and woman could legally be called husband and wife as well as bridegroom and bride. The bride was considered to have been bought by the bridegroom.

After the betrothal (erusin) ceremony, the bridegroom and bride entered a waiting period leading up to the day of the wedding ceremony (which was called "chuppah") just as we have a period of engagement before a modern-day wedding. Between the betrothal (erusin) and wedding ceremony (chuppah), there was typically a period of several months to a year. Once betrothed, the bridegroom would leave his bride at her father's home and go back to his father's home to prepare a place for his new, married life. The bride, for her part, would remain at her father's home and be prepared for the life of a wife. In our day, Jewish people have both ceremonies on the same day, but these events remained separate as late as the Middle Ages.

These two distinctive processes in the marriage were called sanctification or dedication (kiddushin) and actual marriage (nissuin).

Do you see Jesus Christ making a covenant with us? Do you see Him paying with His life, His own blood, to purchase us as His bride? And as He went to be seated at the right hand of the throne of the Father, He said He was going to prepare a place for us that, where He is, we may be also (John 14:2-3). Even now as we wait for His return and the actual marriage, we are being sanctified as the bride, being made ready for the bridegroom, by the Holy Spirit through the ongoing work of Jesus' resurrected life within us.

Brothers and sisters, do you see that we are even now betrothed and in that sanctification period, waiting for our bridegroom to return so that we can enter into the actual marriage of being united with Him through all eternity? Isn't this amazing? He bought and rescued us as His bride. But not only that, He is working through us and letting us participate in the building work He intended and purposed. He is continually sanctifying us with His own blood. And just as an engaged girl excitedly awaits the day when she will always be with her husband, Jesus is to us our All in All, and our all-knowing, all-powerful God. Hallelujah!

God's intention to be Israel's husband is also well known to the Jewish people. In his book *Made in Heaven: A Jewish Wedding Guide*, American Orthodox rabbi Aryeh Kaplan clearly compares the relationship between the bridegroom and bride to the relationship between God and Israel.[1] It is sad that he does not see Jesus as the husband and the church (ekklēsia) as the bride even though Jesus has done everything according to the Jewish traditions and prophecies to fulfill that relationship and the covenant

---

[1] Kaplan, A. (1983). *Made in Heaven: A Jewish Wedding Guide*, Brooklyn: Moznaim Pub Corp.

Jeremiah and Hosea spoke about. However, the book does assert that when the husband and the wife are married, they become one soul.

When we come to Revelation 19, we see the final fulfillment of all these prophecies in glory. We have then come to the wedding ceremony that God intended and purposed all along.

Chapter 8
The Purpose of
the Body of Christ

"Let us rejoice and be glad and give the glory to Him, for the marriage of the Lamb has come and His bride has made herself ready."
Revelation 19:7

The New American Standard Bible has the word "bride" here but some translations have "wife." The Greek word "gynē" can be translated as "woman," "wife," or "bride."

As I wrote earlier, in Jewish custom, once a woman is betrothed to a man, legally she can be called his wife. Since a betrothed bride could be considered a wife, the above verse could be saying that she is the bride, wife, or woman of the Lamb. These are interchangeable. But what we need to see is that she has made herself ready for the marriage of the Lamb, who is our Lord Jesus Christ.

And I saw the holy city, new Jerusalem, coming down out of heaven from God, made ready as a bride adorned for her husband.
Revelation 21:2

As we read further, we see that the holy city, the New Jerusalem is the bride.

Then one of the seven angels who had the seven bowls full of the seven last plagues came and spoke with me, saying, "Come here, I will show you the bride, the wife of the Lamb."
And he carried me away in the Spirit to a great and high mountain, and showed me the holy city, Jerusalem, coming down out of heaven from God,
Revelation 21:9-10

Scripture then describes what the holy city, the New Jerusalem, will be like, including its gates and walls, its measurements, the materials of its construction, and how the glory of God will be the light of the city.

So how does this bride, the holy city, the New Jerusalem make herself ready? Let us read again the verses in Ephesians that speak of God working in and through us to build up the body of Christ.

From whom the whole body, being fitted and held together by what every joint supplies, according to the proper working of each individual part, causes the growth of the body for the building up of itself in love.
Ephesians 4:16

It says that the body of Christ, you and I, the saints of the Lord, builds itself up in love. The word "itself" is the Greek word "heautou" which has meanings of "himself," "herself," "itself," or (plural) "themselves," "yourselves," "ourselves." It is used here to describe His bride who has made herself ready. The body of Christ (which is the church) building itself up in love is like the bride making herself ready for marriage. This mystery is also explained in Ephesians 5 where Paul talks about the relationship between Christ and the church. He explains it as a husband-and-wife relationship, where the two are made one, a relationship that we have become a part of.

For this reason a man shall leave his father and mother and shall be joined to his wife, and the two shall become one flesh. This mystery is great; but I am speaking with reference to Christ and the church.
Ephesians 5:31-32

It is clear that the church (ekklēsia), which is the body of Christ, has to ready itself by being fitted and held together by that which every joint supplies, according to the proper working of each individual part, which causes the growth of the body. By doing this, the church is building itself up in love.

Let's remember that, even though the church is making herself ready, it is God working in and through us that causes the growth. We are only partakers and participants by the grace of God. Praise the Lord who desires us as the body of Christ to be partakers and participants.

It is also by the grace of God that each and every saint is being built together as the spiritual body of Christ, and being prepared as the bride of Christ, which is the holy city, the New Jerusalem. This New Jerusalem is not a city where only God will dwell. Neither is it a city that belongs to this earth. Indeed, it is not being prepared on this earth. Do you remember when Jesus said to store up treasure in heaven, where neither moth nor rust destroys, and where thieves do not break in or steal, and that if our treasure is in heaven, then our hearts will be there also?

This bride, the holy city, the New Jerusalem, is being prepared in heaven. It will someday come down from there to a new heavens and new earth, and so God's dwelling place will be with His people forever. It is our eternal city where God and all the saints will dwell together in eternity. Thus, God's purpose for the body of Christ, which is the church (ekklēsia), is to be prepared as the bride, the holy city, and New Jerusalem. God is not just building a temporary dwelling place where He can meet us, but an eternal dwelling place for all of us to live together with Him forever. And He is building that dwelling place through us. Hallelujah!

For he was looking for the city which has foundations, whose architect and builder is God.
Hebrews 11:10

But as it is, they desire a better country, that is, a heavenly one. Therefore God is not ashamed to be called their God; for He has prepared a city for them.
Hebrews 11:16

But you have come to Mount Zion and to the city of the living God, the heavenly Jerusalem, and to myriads of angels,

Hebrews 12:22

For here we do not have a lasting city, but we are seeking the city which is to come.

Hebrews 13:14

He who overcomes, I will make him a pillar in the temple of My God, and he will not go out from it anymore; and I will write on him the name of My God, and the name of the city of My God, the new Jerusalem, which comes down out of heaven from My God, and My new name.

Revelation 3:12

Then I saw a new heaven and a new earth; for the first heaven and the first earth passed away, and there is no longer any sea. And I saw the holy city, new Jerusalem, coming down out of heaven from God, made ready as a bride adorned for her husband. And I heard a loud voice from the throne, saying, "Behold, the tabernacle of God is among men, and He will dwell among them, and they shall be His people, and God Himself will be among them,

Revelation 21:1-3

For this very purpose, the building of all of us as an eternal dwelling place, God has called us to participate in

His spiritual body. And it is also for this very purpose that we all are being built up as the body of Christ, the church, and prepared as His bride, the New Jerusalem. Can you imagine the love of God desiring to build something like this through us and for us? Can you imagine a greater purpose for our life here on earth? That love of God sent Jesus Christ, who also loved us to the point of death, even though we were enemies of God. If we see the love of God through Jesus Christ, we will have no choice but to change. Let us truly rely on the Holy Spirit so that we will be changed for this amazing purpose of our great God.

If you still cannot imagine how much you are loved, think about the heart of Jesus Christ. He lived a perfect, spotless, and sinless life only to lay it down as He died on the cross for His bride, the church. His body was broken so that all of us could become part of that resurrected spiritual body. He bled till death so that His blood could become the life by which we live. Think about Jesus who laid down His life to take upon Himself the sins of the whole world so that He could gain all of us for Himself. He longs for the day when He returns to claim us as His bride and intercedes for us even today at the right hand of God. That is why we have such a longing for His return, as a bride looks forward to her wedding day. It is the day when the purpose of the body of Christ, God's will and plan, will be fulfilled. Jesus Christ's spiritual body, which is all believers, the church (ekklēsia), is the ark that carries us to be the bride and New Jerusalem, our ultimate dwelling place with God for all eternity.

Chapter 9
How We Should Live

So far we have looked at the Scriptures to see who we are and what we are about. We are the body of Christ which is the church (ekklēsia) and we are about His PURPOSE, that we should be the bride, the New Jerusalem. But perhaps you want to ask, "Now what? What are we supposed to do about this?" My own response is that the Lord has given me a heart that desperately desires to live such a life that I will be participating in what He is doing with the body of

Christ. If we are not able to live our lives for God after examining the Scriptures and seeing and recognizing what He desires, then our study has been of no use.

Then how should we, who have read, seen, and recognized the truth, live our lives? Simply put, we ought to live a life as those who embrace the light of the Lord and let the light shine out from our inner beings as we look forward to His return as a bride who longs for her wedding day. But we have an enemy who knows God's purpose and what He is doing. And even today, as you read this book, he is working to deceive us and to devise a scheme to lead our hearts astray from the sincerity and purity of our devotion to Christ.

For I am jealous for you with a godly jealousy; for I betrothed you to one husband, so that to Christ I might present you as a pure virgin. But I am afraid that, as the serpent deceived Eve by his craftiness, your minds will be led astray from the simplicity and purity of devotion to Christ.
2 Corinthians 11:2-3

All of us who truly believe in Christ belong to the body of Christ. We have been saved by Christ, and through Christ, and were born again into His body. We are followers and disciples of Christ as well as the bride of

Christ. Therefore, we have to make sure our hearts and minds continue to have a simple and pure devotion to Christ. We must remember the Lord by encouraging one another as we await His return.

Does all this mean that we just have to try really hard? Does this mean that we have to be more religious in our outward life? Absolutely not. Our human endeavors and human efforts cannot accomplish anything good in and of themselves. But if we rely on the Lord and His Holy Spirit to help us every day, every moment, I believe that He will lead us and enable us to do everything good in Him. This work will not be accomplished through our trying hard or believing in ourselves that we can do all things. It will be accomplished only because we believe in the Lord and rely on the Holy Spirit inside us to help us and strengthen us. It is only through this kind of faith that we will be able to do all things. This is what it means to live by faith in the Lord.

I can do all things through Him who strengthens me.
　　Philippians 4:13

Today we are taught that if we want something badly enough, try hard enough, and believe in ourselves enough, we will be able to accomplish anything. These worldly ideals of aiming high, being the best we can be, and achieving success flourish in the minds of many (even among Christians), but these concepts aren't in the Bible. The Bible does not say, "Let men live and do the best they can"; rather, "that which is born of the flesh is flesh and that which is born of the Spirit is spirit" (John 3:6). Jesus was very clear on this point.

Jesus answered, "Truly, truly, I say to you, unless one is born of water and the Spirit he cannot enter into the kingdom of God. That which is born of the flesh is flesh, and that which is born of the Spirit is spirit.
John 3:5-6

This is why we must set our minds on things above and not on things of the earth. Instead of walking according to our flesh and carrying out the desire of the flesh, we can walk by the Spirit and carry out the desire of the Spirit. The Bible makes it clear that there is the Spirit as well as the flesh. Since our God is Spirit, not only must we worship Him in spirit and truth, but we must also follow Him in spirit. God's invisible nature has been evident ever since the creation.

For since the creation of the world His invisible attributes, His eternal power and divine nature, have been clearly seen, being understood

through what has been made, so that they are without excuse.
Romans 1:20

Think of the human body. God created our bodies perfectly and exquisitely in His image. Do people live because they want to live? No, people are alive because God is life and He desired to give life to other beings. If we don't have life, it does not matter how much our bodies want to live, we won't be able to live. This is exactly the picture of the body of Christ and us in Him. If we believe in the Lord Jesus Christ as the Bible says, no matter where we are and whatever we are doing, we are alive in the body of Christ by faith. Therefore, we must remember how we were born again into the body of Christ. If we don't have faith in the Lord Jesus Christ, we do not have life.

This is why our enemy Satan continuously attacks our faith; he is a murderer who hates our life and wants to destroy us completely. I said earlier that God's purpose for the body of Christ is that we be prepared as the bride and New Jerusalem. I further say that God's purpose for every individual believer like you and me is for us to be an overcomer until the end by keeping our faith so that we can also be part of the prepared bride and New Jerusalem.

Behind all these purposes, God the Father has a desire to be together with us in eternity. God the Father's desire is waiting for us and always before us.

For momentary, light affliction is producing for us an eternal weight of glory far beyond all comparison, while we look not at the things which are seen, but at the things which are not seen; for the things which are seen are temporal, but the things which are not seen are eternal.

2 Corinthians 4:17-18

And He will wipe away every tear from their eyes; and there will no longer be any death; there will no longer be any mourning, or crying, or pain; the first things have passed away."

Revelation 21:4

We are a people who are looking forward to this eternal life with God forever, who so loves us, and we are called to live a life even now filled with the Spirit of God. We are not to be deceived by the things of this world, but to rely on the Lord Jesus Christ alone as our Source of life. Thank You, Lord Jesus, for giving us Your life to live by!

Chapter 10
How We Should Gather

When I wrote that the buildings people go to on Sundays have nothing to do with being in the body of Christ, I did not mean that gathering with other believers is not important. I meant that the body of Christ is something we are a part of 24 hours a day, 7 days a week, 365 days a year. Once we are in the body of Christ, there is not a moment when we are not part of that body. It is as simple as that. You are either in the body of Christ or you are not. There is no in between. We cannot sometimes be in the body of Christ and other times be apart from it. It is not strictly scriptural to use language like, "going to church on Sunday." Instead, the expressions we find in Scripture are, "when you come together as a church," "when you meet together," "gathered the church together," and "when you assemble." It is not that people have to gather together for there to be a church, but that the believers are the church. Of course, when we are gathered, we are called the church. The word "church" means "assembly," and assembling is something the church does; but biblically, we are always the church, all the time.

In the early days of the church in Jerusalem, believers met daily at the temple and from house to house. Where and when they met did not define who they were. They knew who they were. Therefore, we would not expect any of the early believers in the Book of Acts to say, "Because I go to the temple on most Sundays, I must be a believer in Jesus Christ."

Brothers and sisters, we are either believers or unbelievers. That is how we define whether or not we are part of the body of Christ, which is the church (ekklēsia).

Think about the family you were born into. Did you obtain your membership in your family by meeting together on Sundays? Did you become a member by signing a membership commitment? No, you are in your family because you were born into that family. The moment you became a life, you became a part of that family's life. Whether we see each other every day, once a month or once every ten years, we are still family. On the other hand, because we are family, it is only natural and right that we see each other often to fellowship, to love, and to encourage each other. God's family is the same way. We do not necessarily have to meet or gather to be a family. But to live life as the body of Christ, the family of God, we ought to gather often to fellowship, to love and encourage one other. Because we all love the Lord Jesus and look forward to His return together, we meet and gather. Because we all believe in our Lord Jesus and are one with the same life we share, we meet and gather.

Day by day continuing with one mind in the temple, and breaking bread from house to house, they were taking their meals together with gladness and sincerity of heart, praising God and having favor with all the people. And the Lord was adding to their number day by day those who were being saved.
Acts 2:46-47

This is exactly what we see in the first century church (ekklēsia). In the book of Acts, saints were gathering with gladness and sincerity of heart, praising God and having favor with all the people. Just as Jesus said, "And I, if I am lifted up from the earth, will draw all men to Myself," note that He is drawing people to HIMSELF (John 12:32)—not to a building or a place, but to Himself.

When Jesus Christ was resurrected two thousand years ago, His spiritual body was raised and His church (ekklēsia) has since been growing and building itself up to fulfill His purpose. As Jesus said to the Pharisees, "The kingdom of God is not coming with signs to be observed; nor will they say, 'Look, here it is!' or, 'There it is!' For behold, the kingdom of God is in your midst" (Luke 17:21). Read the following picture Jesus gives us of the kingdom of God:

And He said, "How shall we picture the kingdom of God, or by what parable shall we present it? It is like a mustard seed, which, when sown upon the soil, though it is smaller than all the seeds that are upon the soil, yet when it is sown, it grows up and becomes larger than all the garden plants and forms large branches; so that the birds of the air can nest under its shade."

Mark 4:30-32

As I mentioned in chapter two, we can see that He is giving us a picture of the kingdom of God and the body of Christ, which was sown in a perishable, natural body in dishonor and weakness. But, praise the Lord, He was raised an imperishable, spiritual body in glory and power.

It is sown a perishable body, it is raised an imperishable body; it is sown in dishonor, it is raised in glory; it is sown in weakness, it is raised in power; it is sown a natural body, it is raised a spiritual body. If there is a natural body, there is also a spiritual body.

    1 Corinthians 15:42-44

So, just like the kingdom of God, the body of Christ, which is the church (ekklēsia), is also not preeminently a thing you can see or find to join. We who are saved by faith, who are spiritually alive by being born again, are already a part of the spiritual body of Christ. And we are the church.

We ought to consider the question, "Am I living in faith by the life of Christ?" That determines whether we are in the church (ekklēsia) or not. If we are living by the life of Christ in faith, then we are members of Christ's body and we will be called the church whenever and wherever we are gathered in the name of our Lord Jesus. And let's always remember that even when we are not gathered with other believers, we are still in the body of Christ, which is the church. Our Lord Jesus will always be with all of us who are in the body of Christ. Praise the Lord, who is the Savior of all the saints, who promised that He will be with us always, even to the end of the age.

Then how should we gather as the body of Christ, the church (ekklēsia)? How often should we gather as believers in Christ? Is it wrong to meet regularly on Sundays once a week? Not at all. Am I saying you need to come out of your current church or gathering? Not necessarily. However, if you sense that you are being taught a different gospel from that which is in the Bible, or a different Jesus from the Jesus in the Bible, or forced to follow a man as the Lord, then ask the Holy Spirit what to do. The Holy Spirit who is our Helper and Teacher will guide and direct you as you rely on Him. Boldly ask the Holy Spirit to speak to you about things that are distracting you from your faith, and earnestly pray in the name of Jesus Christ. Walk away from any mere form of godliness without power, mere human tradition, the elementary principles of the world, seeking the favor of men, or anything else that causes you to be in bondage, and instead walk by the Spirit.

It is not buildings or meeting places that we must be freed from, but the obstacles that bind, distract, and disturb our hearts so that we can't be led by the Spirit. If our hearts are in bondage to anything, we will not be free no matter where we are, and if our hearts are free to follow the Lord Jesus, we will be able to walk in the Spirit, no matter where we are. Let's remember, whoever is united with the Lord Jesus is one in spirit with the Lord, and where the Spirit is, there is freedom.

But whenever a person turns to the Lord, the veil is taken away. Now

the Lord is the Spirit, and where the Spirit of the Lord is, there is
liberty.

2 Corinthians 3:16-18

Paul tells us what to do if someone becomes a believer
and has an unbelieving spouse. The Lord does not tell us
to leave that unbelieving spouse to follow Him. The Lord
tells us to follow Him in the condition in which we were
called.

But to the married I give instructions, not I, but the Lord, that the
wife should not leave her husband (but if she does leave, she must
remain unmarried, or else be reconciled to her husband), and that the
husband should not divorce his wife.
But to the rest I say, not the Lord, that if any brother has a wife who
is an unbeliever, and she consents to live with him, he must not divorce
her. And a woman who has an unbelieving husband, and he consents
to live with her, she must not send her husband away. For the
unbelieving husband is sanctified through his wife, and the unbelieving
wife is sanctified through her believing husband; for otherwise your
children are unclean, but now they are holy. Yet if the unbelieving one
leaves, let him leave; the brother or the sister is not under bondage in
such cases, but God has called us to peace. For how do you know, O
wife, whether you will save your husband? Or how do you know, O
husband, whether you will save your wife?

Only, as the Lord has assigned to each one, as God has called each, in this manner let him walk. And so I direct in all the churches.
1 Corinthians 7:10-17

In this passage, the Lord asks how anyone would know whether they will save their unbelieving spouse. In the same way, how can we know what God will do through us in any given circumstance since He is the one who places us? That is the reason we must remain in the condition in which we were called. But Paul is not only talking about marriage with an unbeliever. He is also talking about circumcision. He points out that it is not about being circumcised or uncircumcised, but rather keeping God's commandments. Again, he says that each person must remain in the condition in which he was called.

Was any man called when he was already circumcised? He is not to become uncircumcised. Has anyone been called in uncircumcision? He is not to be circumcised. Circumcision is nothing, and uncircumcision is nothing, but what matters is the keeping of the commandments of God. Each man must remain in that condition in which he was called.
1 Corinthians 7:18-20

These verses are telling us that it is not important how

we have lived or what we have done. What is important is that we keep God's commandments as called ones. It even says not to worry if we were called while we were slaves. While we may be slaves, the truth is that we are the Lord's free men. At the same time, if we are free, we are to be Christ's slaves.

Were you called while a slave? Do not worry about it; but if you are able also to become free, rather do that. For he who was called in the Lord while a slave, is the Lord's freedman; likewise he who was called while free, is Christ's slave. You were bought with a price; do not become slaves of men. Brethren, each one is to remain with God in that condition in which he was called.

1 Corinthians 7:21-24

Our life in the body of Christ is similar. It does not always matter where you are or with whom you gather. We do not necessarily need to go to places that look good and spiritual in our own eyes. What matters is what God wants. If you feel that you have been enslaved to religious mindsets or religious systems, you do not need to worry, but merely seek to dwell with God. If you can be freed, it is better to choose freedom and not be a slave to anything. But the most important thing is that we be with God and keep His commandments. By doing so, we will be able to stand firm in the faith and to hear the voice of the Holy Spirit. And if we stand in the faith and desire to be led by the Spirit, the Lord can move us at any time as He desires.

The question of whether or not we are part of the body of Christ is not primarily based on where we go on Sundays or whom we are meeting with. The key is to be filled with the Holy Spirit and encourage one another, love one another, serve one other, and proclaim the Lord Jesus to all. That is how God causes growth in and through us for the building up of the body of Christ. Please note that such growth is not necessarily numerical but always spiritual.

Does this mean that we don't need to get together regularly as long as we live this way, or that we don't need to consider what sort of group we are meeting with? Not at all. When we consider assembling with others as the church, there are many examples of the church being the assembly of believers in the Bible, and we are encouraged to gather together as the church. Not only does the Bible tell us not to forsake assembling together, but it also says to encourage one another day after day as long as it is still called today. So the point is that we should not focus too much on outward forms, procedures, or rituals. The point is that we have fellowship with one another by the Holy Spirit in the name of our Lord Jesus Christ. If we focus only on outward things, we may miss inward fellowship with one another in the Holy Spirit.

When we consider the question of which church,

which local assembly of believers, we are to be gathered with, we must remember that our God is sovereign. And this must be God's choice, not our choice.

Wherever we are, we must look to our Lord Jesus Christ and hear what His Spirit is saying to us. The Holy Spirit is our Helper, Teacher, and Guide. I truly believe that if we ask the Holy Spirit what we should do, where we should go, and whom we should gather with, our Lord will surely answer and lead us. Our Lord is such a great Shepherd of His sheep. Praise the Lord!

Chapter 11
Why We Gather

I have already mentioned many times (and I don't think I can say it enough) that our gathering together is not what makes us members of the church (ekklēsia), which is the body of Christ. Neither can we suppose that, when we gather, our gathering is the only church. We gather because we are members of the body of Christ and to stimulate one another to love and good deeds. For this reason (and others), the Scripture tells us not to forsake our own assembling together. Our focus is not on attendance in itself or on the gathering's outward format, but rather on encouraging one another and all the more as we see the day drawing near.

And let us consider how to stimulate one another to love and good deeds, not forsaking our own assembling together, as is the habit of some, but encouraging one another; and all the more as you see the day drawing near.

Hebrews 10: 24-25

Before I share more about the reasons why we gather, I want to point out some wrong reasons people gather. We live in a day when many churches operate as businesses, and Scriptures such as Hebrews 10:24-25 are used to bring in more people, fill up the pews, raise more financial offerings, and prosper the church ministries. Indeed, this passage is one of the main Scriptures some pastors and preachers use to insist that believers come to their church so that they can perpetuate their "church business." It is truly sad that many of these church businesses don't even preach the gospel or insist that their new members be born again. It is no surprise that we now have a prosperity gospel that is not the same gospel you see in the Bible, a different Jesus who doesn't talk about sin, and the love of God interpreted to mean that He is okay with willful sin and sinful lifestyles among His people. It is true that all of us are sinners and we can come as sinners to God through the blood of Jesus Christ, but the Bible makes it very clear that we cannot use God's love or Jesus's sacrifice to justify a life of willful sin. If you go on to the next verse, you will read a warning against this very thing.

For if we go on sinning willfully after receiving the knowledge of the truth, there no longer remains a sacrifice for sins, but a terrifying expectation of judgment and the fury of a fire which will consume the adversaries. Anyone who has set aside the Law of Moses dies without mercy on the testimony of two or three witnesses. How much severer punishment do you think he will deserve who has trampled under foot the Son of God, and has regarded as unclean the blood of the covenant by which he was sanctified, and has insulted the Spirit of grace? For we know Him who said, "Vengeance is Mine, I will repay." And again, "The Lord will judge His people." It is a terrifying thing to fall into the hands of the living God.
Hebrews 10:26-31

Thankfully these words will not condemn us if we heed the last verse of the chapter:

But we are not of those who shrink back to destruction, but of those who have faith to the preserving of the soul.
Hebrews 10:39

Yes, we have our Savior and Lord Jesus Christ who died for all our sins—not just for past sins, but present and future sins as well. But we should not be those whose hearts are so ignorant of the intention of God's grace that we willfully sin and justify sin. We should not be those "who turn the grace of God into licentiousness" (Jude 4). We must not shrink back to destruction but have faith to the preserving of our souls until the very end.

The right reason to gather is to stimulate one another to love and good deeds. As the day when our Lord Jesus will return is drawing near, we encourage one another all the more to do those things. As we gather to remember the Lord Jesus, to long for His return, and to love and encourage one another, the body of Christ is being built up in love. This is done by all the saints, after being equipped for every good work, doing the work of service for the building up of the body of Christ. That is why we must come together to equip, to encourage, to remember, to serve, to stimulate, and to love one another.

Someone has said, "We don't work to get saved, we work because we are saved." This is similar to what we have discussed about the body of Christ. We don't gather to become members of the church, we gather because we are members of the church.

Let us look in greater detail at how the body of Christ is being built up so that we can see more clearly what happens in the kingdom of God spiritually when we gather to do all the things mentioned above.

For we are God's fellow workers; you are God's field, God's building. According to the grace of God which was given to me, like a wise master builder I laid a foundation, and another is building on it. But each man must be careful how he builds on it. For no man can lay a foundation other than the one which is laid, which is Jesus Christ. Now if any man builds on the foundation with gold, silver, precious stones, wood, hay, straw, each man's work will become evident; for the day will show it because it is to be revealed with fire, and the fire itself will test the quality of each man's work. If any man's work which he has built on it remains, he will receive a reward. If any man's work is burned up, he will suffer loss; but he himself will be saved, yet so as through fire.

1 Corinthians 3:9-15

Here Paul makes very clear that we are all God's field and God's building. And in the verses right before this passage, he says that he planted and Apollos watered. Obviously, he is not referring to a physical plot of ground, but rather, a field of humanity. In this passage he also speaks of laying the foundation of Jesus Christ. That foundation is laid spiritually in the hearts, souls, and minds of the saints—in their inner man.

We are all God's field and God's building. If we believe in the Lord Jesus as our Savior, we all have the foundation of Jesus Christ in our hearts, souls, and minds. And when we work and take action, we are all building something on that foundation. Clearly, it is better to build with gold, silver, and precious stones than with wood, hay and straw.

And make no mistake: we are always cultivating something in the field; we are always building something in our hearts, souls, and minds, in our inner man. We are also building on each other's hearts, souls, and minds. When we patiently love and encourage one another, that patience, love, and encouragement turn into building materials such as gold, silver, and precious stones.

This building work does not happen only on Sundays. Being built together should not be defined by Sunday mornings or confined to certain people you see on Sundays. If you have been thinking that Sunday is the day that all this building work happens, ask the Holy Spirit to reveal the truth to you right now. If you have been thinking only certain people you see on Sundays are being built together, you need a larger vision of the body of Christ, and to see how big the spiritual body of our Lord Jesus is, and how God may use anyone anywhere to build that body.

Our God is infinitely great and does not use Sundays only to build. Neither is He limited to the people you recognize around you when it comes to building up the body of Christ.

If you are with other believers who already have a solid foundation of Christ, then you can build on one another. Perhaps you are in a place where you don't sense the foundation of Jesus in people around you. It may be that He wants you there to share the gospel and to be a laborer working to lay the foundation of Jesus Christ. I so eagerly desire these things to happen at every moment, everywhere, because by these things the body of Christ is being built up and the bride prepared. This is why our life as the members of the body of Christ, the church (ekklēsia), has to be our daily life. And to stimulate one another to live such a life, we ought to gather as often as we can.

We proclaim Him, admonishing every man and teaching every man with all wisdom, so that we may present every man complete in Christ. For this purpose also I labor, striving according to His power, which mightily works within me.
Colossians 1:28-29

Here in the book of Colossians, Paul says that he is admonishing and teaching men with all wisdom because he wants to present every man complete in Christ. Paul also says that his labor is according to Christ's power which mightily works within him. In other words, Paul is laboring in this work with gold, silver, and precious stones to build up the body of Christ. I want to emphasize again that we are not, in and of ourselves, the ones who are doing the work. It is God doing it through us. Paul makes this point again by saying it is according to Christ's power which mightily works within him. Let us look to the Lord our God who works mightily in us to cause us to participate in what He is doing. If we do man's work according to man's strength and man's desire, it will all burn up in the fiery test on the last day. Only what God has done through man will remain.

And here is one thing we must not miss: All this building work that God is doing in us is to prepare the bride that is the New Jerusalem in the heavenly realm of the spirit. Therefore, none of what the Lord has done in and through us for the building of that heavenly city can be lost. Paul wrote in 1 Corinthians that if any man's work which he has built remains, through the testing of fire, he will receive a reward. If what he built was by God's working and using the Lord's gold, silver, and precious stones, he will not suffer loss. This is so freeing, and I'm thankful for the great assurance that God has given us.

Here is an example: I can build in my family with such precious things as patience, love, joy, peace, encouragement, and other fruits of the Spirit. But if our home relationship suddenly changed for the worse, the earlier building work would seem in vain. From an earthly point of view, we would say things went south and aren't so good anymore for our family. But in the eternal construction work of the New Jerusalem, if we have built something through the working of God, it will survive the testing of fire, and we will be rewarded. This means we don't have to focus just on the outcome of our lives, but we can focus also on every detail of our lives without worrying that our true and heavenly work will be for nothing. As long as we work as the Lord causes us to, we can work in faith that our work in Him will not be in vain.

Here is an example from my own personal experience. When there are dear brothers and sisters whom you loved and encouraged, but now the situation is such that you cannot meet with each other, you may feel pain as if some part of you has been torn to pieces. You also may feel as though the work of God that you met with, loved, encouraged, and built together is now utterly broken and lying in ruins. But our faithful God does not allow the body of Christ, the bride, or the New Jerusalem to be spoiled or to fall eternally. God's purpose is not destroyed by our or others' mistakes or failures because He keeps all the building work that has been done with gold, silver, and precious stones in heaven where moth and rust cannot destroy and thieves cannot steal. It may be painful and sad in this earthly realm, but we ought to remember that the work of the Lord and the purpose of everything is in heaven, in the bride which is the New Jerusalem. No matter how unstable and insecure things may look here on earth; in heaven the work is done in glory day by day, and being completed daily, and we are right now very near to the completion of that work.

Let us praise God who is working in and through us to build His eternal purpose and who is also safeguarding everything in heaven. Let us live our daily lives as workers and servants of the Lord Jesus Christ in boldness, believing that this great and perfect God will not allow our work to be in vain.

But thanks be to God, who gives us the victory through our Lord Jesus Christ. Therefore, my beloved brethren, be steadfast, immovable, always abounding in the work of the Lord, knowing that your toil is not in vain in the Lord.

1 Corinthians 15:57-58

Chapter 12
Ekklēsia: Awake, Arise, Shine

"Arise, shine; for your light has come,
And the glory of the LORD has risen upon you.
"For behold, darkness will cover the earth
And deep darkness the peoples;
But the LORD will rise upon you
And His glory will appear upon you.
"Nations will come to your light,
And kings to the brightness of your rising.

"Lift up your eyes round about and see;
They all gather together, they come to you.
Your sons will come from afar,
And your daughters will be carried in the arms.
"Then you will see and be radiant,
And your heart will thrill and rejoice;
Because the abundance of the sea will be turned to you,
The wealth of the nations will come to you.
Isaiah 60:1-5

As we come to the close of this book, I want to shout from the housetops: "Ekklēsia: wake up, arise, and shine!" As we wait on the Lord Jesus' soon return, we need to prepare ourselves and one another to be the hands and feet of the body of Christ! I call upon all who are in the body of Christ, which is the church, the ekklēsia (God's household, family, people, descendants, flock, and sheep) to be awake and ready. Let all of us raise one voice as the bride and say, "Come, Lord Jesus!"

Where and how do we do that? As I mentioned earlier, it is not about where we are physically. It is our inner man that needs to awake, arise, and shine. You can stay right where you are reading this book and do all three of these things. None of these requires your physical action initially, but your heart, soul, and mind must be moved. You can go to as many "church services" or "Christian gatherings" as you like, but unless your heart, soul, and mind are moved, you are not awake and therefore cannot rise to shine. I believe this is why the greatest commandment of the Law concerns the heart, soul, and mind.

"Teacher, which is the great commandment in the Law?" And He said to him, "'You shall love the Lord your God with all your heart, and with all your soul, and with all your mind.' This is the great and foremost commandment.
Matthew 22:36-38

I encourage you to awake, arise, and shine from where you are. Let the Spirit of God lead and direct you to do all things so as to please the Lord.

To reiterate: what is most important is not outward and physical matters such as where we go or what we do. The state of our heart, soul, and mind is central. And with that understanding, I would like to share one last warning.

For you were called to freedom, brethren; only do not turn your freedom into an opportunity for the flesh, but through love serve one another. For the whole Law is fulfilled in one word, in the statement, "You shall love your neighbor as yourself." But if you bite and devour one another, take care that you are not consumed by one another.

But I say, walk by the Spirit, and you will not carry out the desire of the flesh. For the flesh sets its desire against the Spirit, and the Spirit against the flesh; for these are in opposition to one another, so that you may not do the things that you please. But if you are led by the Spirit, you are not under the Law. Now the deeds of the flesh are evident, which are: immorality, impurity, sensuality, idolatry, sorcery, enmities, strife, jealousy, outbursts of anger, disputes, dissensions, factions, envying, drunkenness, carousing, and things like these, of which I forewarn you, just as I have forewarned you, that those who practice such things will not inherit the kingdom of God. But the fruit of the Spirit is love, joy, peace, patience, kindness, goodness, faithfulness, gentleness, self-control; against such things there is no law. Now those who belong to Christ Jesus have crucified the flesh with its passions and desires.

If we live by the Spirit, let us also walk by the Spirit. Let us not become boastful, challenging one another, envying one another.

Galatians 5:13-26

There is a so-called "Christianity" in this generation that pursues what seems right in its own eyes. While it is true that Christ has set us free, it was not so we could turn our freedom into an opportunity for the flesh and its desires. It was so we could turn our freedom into an opportunity for the Spirit to produce the fruit of the Spirit in us, which is love, joy, peace, patience, kindness, goodness, faithfulness, gentleness, and self-control. And it was for

Jesus Christ's purpose and plan that we are set free.

When I say that it is not about our going to "church services" or "Christian gatherings" but rather being the body of Christ by faith, I don't mean that we don't need to gather or that we can go anywhere anytime we like. When I say our physical and outward actions are not required to awake, arise, and shine, I don't mean that we don't need to do anything physical or outward. I mean that our focus shouldn't be on the outward and physical, but rather on the inward and the heart, and being led by the Lord. I mean that we must turn to the Lord with our hearts, souls, and minds and not just be going places or doing things.

Is it right for me only to look for and meet with believers who have similar teachings, minds, and preferences to mine and approve only them as the church (ekklēsia)? How about seeking a certain style of worship or looking for music we like? Do we decide to "join" only certain churches because they have what we desire? Is finding the right place that we call "the church" only for our benefit, or is it for the Lord to gain what He desires through His people? Recently, I learned a new word: "churchianity," that speaks of a so-called Christianity focusing more on church life and experience than theology and spiritual life. We live in a day when people church shop to fulfill their desires and tastes. We also have many church businesses in competition with each other to draw more members by catering to people's wants and desires. The body of Christ, the true church, however, is not about our experiences or tastes. It is not about us and what we like or dislike. It is about Him being with us and fulfilling His purpose in and through us.

Someone may ask, if good things are happening and people are being helped, what is wrong with supporting a church business or churchianity? It is wrong because it distracts us from that which is most important. What is most important is the condition of our hearts, souls, and minds. Church businesses and churchianity focused primarily on people's experiences and their own growth tend towards self-centeredness rather than God-centeredness. In some cases, the tragic result will be that people are trained to entertain and worship themselves rather than God. Such churches become human-centered organizations. It ought not be this way. As we gather as the ekklēsia, God must be our life, our absolute center, our everything.

I believe the following passage is crucial to our understanding of the body of Christ. Please consider what these verses say:

For the body is not one member, but many. If the foot says, "Because I am not a hand, I am not a part of the body," it is not for this reason any the less a part of the body. And if the ear says, "Because I am not an eye, I am not a part of the body," it is not for this reason any the less a part of the body. If the whole body were an eye, where would the hearing be? If the whole were hearing, where would the sense of smell be? But now God has placed the members, each one of them, in the body, just as He desired. If they were all one member, where would the body be? But now there are many members, but one body. And the eye cannot say to the hand, "I have no need of you"; or again the head to the feet, "I have no need of you." On the contrary, it is much truer that the members of the body which seem to be weaker are necessary; and those members of the body which we deem less honorable, on these we bestow more abundant honor, and our less presentable members become much more presentable, whereas our more presentable members have no need of it. But God has so composed the body, giving more abundant honor to that member which lacked, so that there may be no division in the body, but that the members may have the same care for one another. And if one member suffers, all the members suffer with it; if one member is honored, all the members rejoice with it. Now you are Christ's body, and individually members of it. And God has appointed in the church, first apostles, second prophets, third teachers, then miracles, then gifts of healings, helps, administrations, various kinds of tongues. All are not apostles, are they? All are not prophets, are they? All are not teachers, are they? All are not workers of miracles, are they? All do not have gifts of healings, do they? All do not speak with tongues, do they? All do not interpret, do they? But earnestly desire the greater gifts. And I show you a still more excellent way.

1 Corinthians 12:14-31

We know that this "more excellent way" in the next

chapter is love. Even as we are told that these three: faith, hope, and love remain, Paul says that the greatest of these is love. With this gift of love, we can be workers in the body of Christ, the church (ekklēsia). If you don't feel that you have love for your brothers and sisters in Christ, then you can earnestly desire the gift of love.

It is so important that we remember the body of Christ is not being built up by only a few people. It is built up by every saint, you and me included. This is why we need to be equipped so that we can serve one another. As we do so, the Lord is letting us participate in His purpose. Our first mission field is our own heart, soul, and mind, then our family and neighbors, and ultimately all those we come across by the Lord's leading are our mission fields where we can love and encourage. Our mission is not on any particular day or in any particular place, but rather it is discovered daily as we walk by the Spirit of God.

"When the Most High gave the nations their inheritance,
When He separated the sons of man,
He set the boundaries of the peoples
According to the number of the sons of Israel.
Deuteronomy 32:8

And He made from one man every nation of mankind to live on all the face of the earth, having determined their appointed times and the

boundaries of their habitation,
    Acts 17:26

    Brothers and sisters, do you see that we are where God wants us and already in God's mission fields, which are in us and all around us? May we be awake in every place God has placed us, to call upon the name of the Lord, and to let the Holy Spirit lead so that we may walk and do all things according to His purpose. Our God is working, guiding, and leading us all, not only on Sundays and not only in "church" buildings, but everywhere through everything. Praise the Lord, the Almighty!

So ekklēsia: awake, arise, and shine wherever you are.

You are the light of the world. A city set on a hill cannot be hidden; nor does anyone light a lamp and put it under a basket, but on the lampstand, and it gives light to all who are in the house. Let your light shine before men in such a way that they may see your good works, and glorify your Father who is in heaven.
    Matthew 5:14-16

As I Finish This Book

My one and only hobby while visiting Korea in 2018 was reading Christians books in used bookstores. I did this because I had already started to write this book and was curious what the Holy Spirit was speaking to other saints in Korea. I must say that I was shocked to see so many Christian books in secular bookstores. These days there is no lack of knowledge, information, or teaching.

If we lack anything, we lack in hearing what the Holy

Spirit is saying to the churches. We lack the power of the Holy Spirit in many Christians' lives. We lack being filled with the Holy Spirit to do every good work God has for us to do. Obviously, it is only by the Holy Spirit that we can hear what the Spirit is saying to the churches. And it is only by being filled with the Holy Spirit that we can do all things through Him.

It is my prayer that this book would not express my ideas, beliefs, theology, or thought, but rather that the work of the Holy Spirit would fill this book. I pray that every last person who reads this book will be filled with the Spirit of God to live life in Christ Jesus day by day.

Now these were more noble-minded than those in Thessalonica, for they received the word with great eagerness, examining the Scriptures daily to see whether these things were so. Therefore many of them believed, along with a number of prominent Greek women and men.
Acts 17:11-12

Here in Acts 17, many of the Bereans came to faith because they received the word with great eagerness and examined the Scriptures daily. I am sure that if we become eager to hear what the Spirit is saying and continue to meditate on the Word of God as they did, we will be able to hear the Spirit and to bring much glory to the Lord. And let us remember that our Lord may be standing outside the door knocking right now. Over and over, He said, "He who has an ear, let him hear what the Spirit says to the churches" (Revelation 2:29).

Brothers and sisters, let us not just "go to church" on Sundays. Let us be the church every day of the week, simply by living out who we are in Christ and being the hands and feet of our Lord Jesus' body on earth. Let us yield our lives to Christ so that He can shine His light more brightly through us as we gather. Whenever and wherever we gather, let's gather with gladness and sincerity to worship Him in spirit and truth. Our Lord Jesus made it possible for us to gather freely in His name, to love and encourage each other to be a part of His eternal purpose. Let us stand firm in our freedom to follow Christ Jesus and to love Him, who is our bridegroom, with all our hearts, continually longing for His soon return. May all of us who are the bride look forward eagerly to His appearing. O Lord Jesus, please come quickly!

"And behold, I am coming quickly. Blessed is he who heeds the words of the prophecy of this book."

"Behold, I am coming quickly, and My reward is with Me, to render to every man according to what he has done."

The Spirit and the bride say, "Come." And let the one who hears say, "Come." And let the one who is thirsty come; let the one who wishes take the water of life without cost."

He who testifies to these things says, "Yes, I am coming quickly." Amen. Come, Lord Jesus.

Revelation 22:7,12,17,20

A Thankful Heart

There is a reason I have placed this note at the end of the book instead of in the "Acknowledgements" at the front. It is because this book is written as a letter to my brothers and sisters in the body of Christ. So I wanted to wait till the end to recognize all those I am thankful for. I have much thankfulness in my heart for the completion of this book (or letter). Throughout this process, I have received much support, encouragement, blessing, and love.

First of all, I thank the Lord Jesus Christ for everything from start to finish. Without Him, nothing would make sense. He is truly the Alpha and the Omega, the first and the last, the beginning and the end, as well as our Savior and bridegroom. Thank You, Lord!

I am very thankful for my loving wife Mina, my dear sister and fellow worker in the Lord. I am always overwhelmingly thankful for her love and support as well as her heart for the Lord. She is always an encouragement and brings healing to my weaknesses. Thank you, honey, for being a home for me.

And thank You Lord for my four wonderful children who each love the Lord Jesus according to their capacity (they are ten, eight, five, and three years old). Through them, I can understand more of the Father's heart for His children. If I love my children so much that I miss them even when I am with them, it makes sense that our heavenly Father would want to be with His children forever in eternity. Thank you, Jacob, Joshua, Julia, and Joseph, for making me so pleased with everything you are to me. I hope to be as pleasing a son to my heavenly Father as you guys are to me.

Thank you, Mom, (and Dad for letting her) for helping me so much with all the process this book went through.

From English to Korean, and from Korean back to English, you were so willing and supportive in everything. I know it is not just because I am your son, but because of your heart for the Lord (which I am the more thankful for).

Thank you, Sol and Dan, for your willingness to help with the Korean translation of the book, the cover design, and all other things. You guys were willing to help with anything I asked for.

Mark, thank you for taking the time to help me make much needed corrections. Your detailed and thorough editorial help as well as spiritual insight made this book complete.

Also, many thanks to Everett for his editing work, without which this book would not read as smoothly. You are an amazing professor.

Thank you, Matt, for all your help in the proofreading and final checking of this book. I am always thankful for your encouragement and leading by example.

To my family in general: thank you. Whether in Memphis, Korea, Beijing, Minnesota, Seattle, Atlanta, or wherever we are, I am thankful that we are family.

Thank you, brothers and sisters who are meeting house to house in Memphis. I am thankful for so much fellowship in the Lord and so much building one another up in the Lord. May we press on. May we stimulate one another to love and good deeds for His purpose.

Much thanks to all the brothers and sisters in Memphis whom the Lord has used over the years to build Christ in me—many whom I see often (if you see me regularly, that's you) and many whom I don't see as often these days. We are all one in the body of Christ wherever we are, dear ones! Let's pursue Christ Jesus together even if physically apart. All of us are for Him and His purpose.

I also want to thank all the brothers and sisters in Korea whom I dearly miss. Thank you, my father-in-law in Korea, for being a father to me. Thank you, brother Namsoo, for all your help and support in Korea (also in spirit). Also, thank you to my Aunt PyungAe, a dear sister in the Lord, for all your work and encouragement. And to many dear saints who love the Lord in Korea, we miss you all in the Lord.

And last, thank you for reading this book. May the Lord bless you greatly so that we can all turn our hearts to Him and together give all glory to Him. He is worthy of it all!

This is now, beloved, the second letter I am writing to you in which I am stirring up your sincere mind by way of reminder, that you should remember the words spoken beforehand by the holy prophets and the commandment of the Lord and Savior spoken by your apostles.

Know this first of all, that in the last days mockers will come with their mocking, following after their own lusts, and saying, "Where is the promise of His coming? For ever since the fathers fell asleep, all continues just as it was from the beginning of creation." For when they maintain this, it escapes their notice that by the word of God the heavens existed long ago and the earth was formed out of water and by water, through which the world at that time was destroyed, being flooded with water. But by His word the present heavens and earth are being reserved for fire, kept for the day of judgment and destruction of ungodly men.

But do not let this one fact escape your notice, beloved, that with the Lord one day is like a thousand years, and a thousand years like one day. The Lord is not slow about His promise, as some count slowness, but is patient toward you, not wishing for any to perish but for all to come to repentance.

But the day of the Lord will come like a thief, in which the heavens will pass away with a roar and the elements will be destroyed with intense heat, and the earth and its works will be burned up.

Since all these things are to be destroyed in this way, what sort of people ought you to be in holy conduct and godliness, looking for and hastening the coming of the day of God, because of which the heavens will be destroyed by burning, and the elements will melt with intense heat! But according to His promise we are looking for new heavens and a new earth, in which righteousness dwells.

Therefore, beloved, since you look for these things, be diligent to be found by Him in peace, spotless and blameless, and regard the patience of our Lord as salvation; just as also our beloved brother Paul, according to the wisdom given him, wrote to you, as also in all his letters, speaking in them of these things, in which are some things hard to understand, which the untaught and unstable distort, as they do also the rest of the Scriptures, to their own destruction. You therefore, beloved, knowing this beforehand, be on your guard so that you are not carried away by the error of unprincipled men and fall from your own steadfastness, but grow in the grace and knowledge of our Lord and Savior Jesus Christ. To Him be the glory, both now and to the day of eternity. Amen.

2 Peter 3

His Ekklēsia,
the body of Christ,
let us raise one unified voice:

Come, Lord Jesus!

Made in the USA
Columbia, SC
24 February 2020